RYA Inte
Re
for Preventing
Collisions at Sea

by Tim Bartlett FRIN

Technical Editor Paul Mara

Foreword James Stevens FRIN

Reprinted March 2010

Reprinted July 2011

Reprinted September 2013

Reprinted August 2014

First Published 2009
The Royal Yachting Association
RYA House, Ensign Way, Hamble,
Southampton SO31 4YA
Tel: 0844 556 9555
Fax: 0844 556 9516
Email: publications@rya.org.uk
Web: www.rya.org.uk
Follow us on Twitter @RYAPublications or on YouTube
ISBN: 978-1906435-196
RYA Order Code: G2

A CIP record of this book is available from the British Library

Cover: Creativebyte
Typeset: Creativebyte
Proofreading and Index: Alan Thatcher
Printed in China through: World Print

Foreword

The right time to start reading this book is long before you are confronted by a vessel on a collision course, or before you encounter a combination of lights at sea which could be a tug complete with towline.

Few maritime rules have been studied as assiduously as the International Regulations for Preventing Collisions at Sea. Every professional mariner from ship's captain to yacht skipper is required to know these, and if found wanting, can face not only danger afloat but also difficult questions in court or an RYA disciplinary tribunal.

Recreational yachtsmen and powerboaters also need to know the rules and be able to act on them "in ample time and with due regard to the observance of good seamanship".

I first learned these when I took a RYA shorebased course, with the motivation of a subsequent test, but there have been plenty of occasions at sea when I am glad I did so. Passage making can be hard enough without wondering what type of vessel is ahead and what it might do.

The rules have been written for mariners by mariners, and coupled with Tim Bartlett's clear text provide an authoritative and clear explanation of this vital maritime subject. The greater the number of seafarers who understand the contents of this book, the safer the sea will be.

James Stevens FRIN
Former RYA Chief Examiner

Contents

Contents

Introduction

No-one, in their right mind, would set out on the road without at least some knowledge of the Highway Code. Even pedestrians need more than an instinct for self-preservation. A strategy of "keep out of the way of everything that moves" may seem foolproof enough, but to apply it, you still need to know that we drive on the left and that vehicles have white lights at the front and red lights at the back.

It's just the same on the water: anyone who takes charge of any vessel – even the smallest canoe or dinghy – needs a basic knowledge of how to react when they meet other water users. Those who operate larger, faster and more potentially-damaging vessels need a correspondingly deeper understanding of the rules that govern more complex situations.

Maybe that seems obvious, now, but it wasn't always the case. The idea of a set of International Regulations for Preventing Collisions at Sea didn't catch on until the latter half of the nineteenth century, and the current rules – often known as IRPCS or "the Colregs" – didn't come into force until 1977. They've been tweaked and amended several times since then, to cope with changing conditions and advancing technology, but some of the most important rules are effectively unchanged from those that were originally agreed between Britain and France, back in 1863.

Although the International Regulations for Preventing Collisions at Sea are widely regarded as "International law", that is, itself, something of an oversimplification. The Colregs are part of an international convention that is binding only on the 150 national governments that have signed up to it – not on individual skippers or owners. But a key part of the convention is that each of those governments has agreed to include the Colregs in their own national legislation. So if the skipper of a British vessel is caught breaking the rules, he could be prosecuted under The Merchant Shipping (Distress Signals and Prevention of Collisions) Regulations 1996.

How to use this book

The full text of the rules runs to almost fifteen thousand words: it is clearly too much for most people to commit to memory!

But relying on simple paraphrases can be misleading: the old chestnut that "power gives way to sail", for instance, is subject to so many exceptions that it is dangerous to rely on it.

So we've split the rules into groups, dealing with them in a sequence that roughly corresponds with the order in which they are most likely to be applied in practice. In each group, we've given the full text of the official rules; and a discussion of some of the most significant points.

Illustrations

The manoeuvring illustrations in this book are not to scale. In most cases, the sizes of vessels are greatly exaggerated for the sake of clarity. Thus an illustration which shows two motor cruisers apparently passing approximately one boat length apart represents a situation in which they would expect to pass at least 100 metres apart in real life.

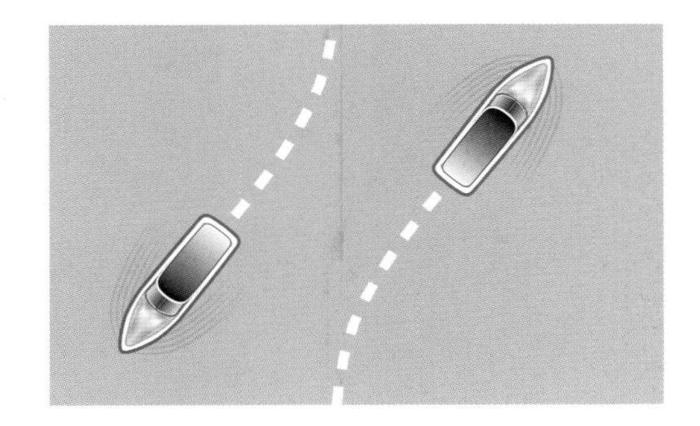

1: Who, where, when?

Rules that always apply

Rule 1: Application

Rule 1: Application

(a) These Rules shall apply to all vessels upon the high seas and in all waters connected therewith navigable by seagoing vessels.

(b) Nothing in these Rules shall interfere with the operation of special rules made by an appropriate authority for roadsteads, harbours, rivers, lakes or inland waterways connected with the high seas and navigable by seagoing vessels. Such special rules shall conform as closely as possible to these Rules.

(c) Nothing in these Rules shall interfere with the operation of any special rules made by the Government of any State with respect to additional station or signal lights, shapes or whistle signals for ships of war and vessels proceeding under convoy, or with respect to additional station or signal lights or shapes for fishing vessels engaged in fishing as a fleet. These additional station or signal lights, shapes or whistle signals shall, so far as possible, be such that they cannot be mistaken for any light, shape or signal authorised elsewhere under these Rules.

(d) Traffic separation schemes may be adopted by the Organization for the purpose of these Rules.

(e) Whenever the Government concerned shall have determined that a vessel of any special construction or purpose cannot comply with the provisions of any of these Rules with respect to the number, position, range or arc of visibility of lights or shapes, as well as to the disposition and characteristics of sound signalling appliances, such vessel shall comply with such other provisions in regard to the number, position, range or arc of visibility of lights or shapes, as well as to the disposition and characteristics of sound signalling appliances, as her Government shall have determined to be the closest possible compliance with these Rules in respect of that vessel.

The first paragraph is self-explanatory: if you're in any kind of vessel, on any piece of water that is connected to the sea, the Colregs apply to you. There are odd loopholes – but the intention is clear.

The later paragraphs are much more wordy, but their meanings are simple enough: governments and local authorities can make their own rules to cope with particular circumstances.

This allows governments to bend the rules for vessels such as submarines that cannot possibly conform to the rules about navigation lights, and to add additional rules for special circumstances.

Local regulations may supplement the Colregs, but should not conflict with them.

It also allows harbour authorities to introduce speed limits, to designate particular channels and exclusion zones, and create local regulations such as the bye-laws that give the Poole chain ferry right of way over all vessels, while its counterpart in Cowes – just twenty five miles to the east – has to give way to everyone!

Unfortunately, many of these local rules are not well publicised.

Some of them appear in official publications such as Admiralty Sailing Directions, and some are mentioned in yachtsmen's pilots and almanacs, but neither of these sources can be relied upon as being entirely comprehensive or up to date. That is why, as a matter of practicality, paragraphs b, c, and e all require such "special rules" to "conform as closely as possible to these Rules".

Rule 2: Responsibility

Rule 2: Responsibility

(a) Nothing in these Rules shall exonerate any vessel, or the owner, master or crew thereof, from the consequences of any neglect to comply with these Rules or of the neglect of any precaution which may be required by the ordinary practice of seamen, or by the special circumstances of the case.

(b) In construing and complying with these Rules due regard shall be had to all dangers of navigation and collision and to any special circumstances, including the limitations of the vessels involved, which may make a departure from these Rules necessary to avoid immediate danger.

In an age in which legislation is becoming ever more prescriptive, there is something delightfully Victorian about Rule 2, which says that rules are no substitute for seamanship or common sense, and if the circumstances of a particular situation would make it dangerous to follow the letter of the rules, you are not merely justified in departing from them, but are required to do so.

For instance, although the Colregs do not give any special status to a vessel at anchor, it would obviously be ridiculous to drive into the side of an anchored vessel and then blame it for not giving way.

A slightly more complicated situation in which Rule 2 applies is shown in the illustration on page 8.

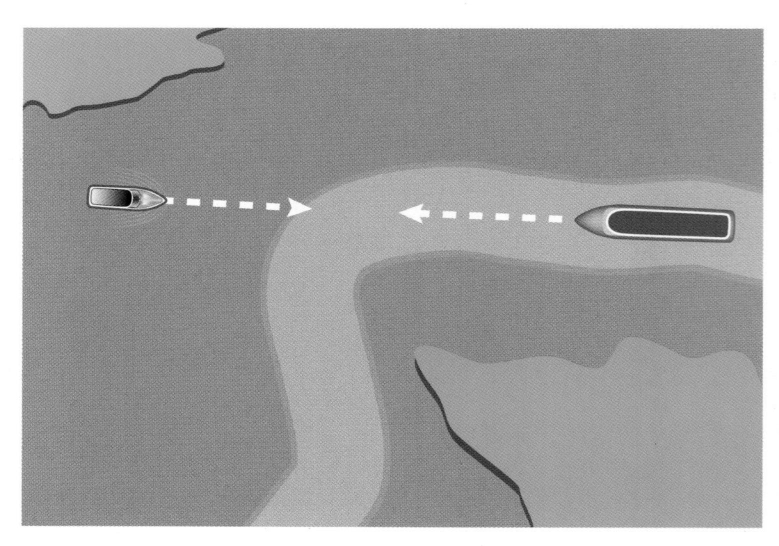

In the illustration, two power-driven vessels are approaching each other head on. One of the best-known rules of all is Rule 14 (page 22), which says that both vessels should alter course to starboard. But in this case, the bend in the deep channel is forcing the larger vessel to turn to port. If the smaller vessel turned to starboard, it would soon find itself on a potential collision course again. It would be much better if the smaller vessel altered course to port – staying out of the deep channel and leaving plenty of room for the larger vessel to negotiate the bend. Rule 2 makes this sensible option legitimate.

Rule 2 does not, however, give anyone carte blanche to bend or break the rules just because they feel like it or because it is convenient to do so. So if two ferries meet head on and agree to reverse Rule 14 by passing "green-to-green" (both altering course to port, instead of starboard), the fact that they may have discussed the manoeuvre by radio is irrelevant: their action would only be legitimate if it were "necessary to avoid immediate danger".

Rule 3: Definitions

Rule 3: General definitions

For the purpose of these Rules, except where the context otherwise requires:

(a) The word "vessel" includes every description of water craft, including non-displacement craft, WIG craft and seaplanes, used or capable of being used as a means of transportation on water.

(b) The term "power-driven vessel" means any vessel propelled by machinery.

(c) The term "sailing vessel" means any vessel under sail provided that propelling machinery, if fitted, is not being used.

(d) The term "vessel engaged in fishing" means any vessel fishing with nets, lines, trawls or other fishing apparatus which restrict manoeuvrability, but does not include a vessel fishing with trolling lines or other fishing apparatus which do not restrict manoeuvrability.

(e) The word "seaplane" includes any aircraft designed to manoeuvre on the water.

(f) The term "vessel not under command" means a vessel which through some exceptional circumstance is unable to manoeuvre as required by these Rules and is therefore unable to keep out of the way of another vessel.

(g) The term "vessel restricted in her ability to manoeuvre" means a vessel which from the nature of her work is restricted in her ability to manoeuvre as required by these Rules and is therefore unable to keep out of the way of another vessel. The term "vessels restricted in their ability to manoeuvre" shall include but not be limited to:
   (i) a vessel engaged in laying, servicing or picking up a navigation mark, submarine cable or pipeline;
   (ii) a vessel engaged in dredging, surveying or underwater operations;
   (iii) a vessel engaged in replenishment or transferring persons, provisions or cargo while underway;
   (iv) a vessel engaged in the launching or recovery of aircraft;
   (v) a vessel engaged in mine clearance operations;
   (vi) a vessel engaged in a towing operation such as severely restricts the towing vessel and her tow in their ability to deviate from their course.

(h) The term "vessel constrained by her draught" means a power-driven vessel which, because of her draught in relation to the available depth and width of navigable water, is severely restricted in her ability to deviate from the course she is following.

(i) The word "underway" means that a vessel is not at anchor, or made fast to the shore, or aground.

(j) The words "length" and "breadth" of a vessel mean her length overall and greatest breadth.

(k) Vessels shall be deemed to be in sight of one another only when one can be observed visually from the other.

(l) The term "restricted visibility" means any condition in which visibility is restricted by fog, mist, falling snow, heavy rainstorms, sandstorms or any other similar causes.

(m) The term "Wing in Ground effect (WIG) craft" means a multimodal craft which, in its main operational mode, flies in close proximity to the surface by utilizing surface-effect action.

Vessels which are restricted in their ability to manoeuvre are given special status in the collision regulations.

The definitions in this rule are largely self-explanatory, but it is important to note that a vessel's "status" under the collision regulations depends on whether its ability to manoeuvre is significantly restricted by what it is actually doing – not on what it was designed to do or intends to do.

So a fishing boat is only a "vessel engaged in fishing" when she is actually using fishing gear that restricts her ability to manoeuvre. She is not "engaged in fishing" when she is bashing home from the fishing grounds, nor when she has been chartered by a party of sea anglers.

By the same token, a sailing vessel only acquires the rights and responsibilities of a "sailing vessel" when she is actually sailing: if the engine is being used – even for "motor-sailing" – she is a "power-driven vessel".

2: Assessing the Risk
Rules that always apply

Part B (Section 1) of the Collision Regulations is called the *"Steering and Sailing Rules"*.

It's probably the most interesting bit, and it is certainly the part that includes the rules that everyone most needs to know. It's divided into three sections, each of which begins with a short and rather obvious rule, such as Rule 4, which kicks off the first section subtitled *"Conduct of vessels in any condition of visibility":-*

Rule 4: Application

Rule 4: Application
Rules in this section apply in any condition of visibility.

Rule 4 applies to:
Rule 5: Look-out (see page 10)
Rule 6: Safe speed (see page 15)
Rule 7: Risk of collision (see page 12)
Rule 8: Action to avoid collision (see page 26)
Rule 9: Narrow channels (see page 31)
and Rule 10: Traffic separation schemes (see page 34)

Rule 5: Look-out

Rule 5: Look-out
"Every vessel shall at all times maintain a proper look-out by sight and hearing as well as by all available means appropriate in the prevailing circumstances and conditions so as to make a full appraisal of the situation and of the risk of collision."

You can't hope to avoid something if you don't know it's there, so without this rule, the other rules might as well not exist. And yet, despite its obvious importance, over 40% of collisions are caused by failure to maintain a proper look-out – more than by any other single cause.

Professional seafarers have collided with each other while going to the toilet, making tea, and dealing with paperwork. Two fishing boats collided while the skipper of the one that should have given way was busy taking his echo sounder to bits, while another ploughed into an anchored tanker because the watchkeeper was watching the television.

A "proper look-out"

The meaning of "a proper look-out" is written into the rule itself: it means a look-out that provides all the information required to make "a full appraisal of the situation". Whether that includes radar, radio, or AIS is far less obvious.

In daylight and clear visibility, radar might add very little to your understanding of the situation, and would probably not affect your assessment of the risk of collision. And in a sailing yacht, in particular, there is a lot to be said for saving power during daylight hours in order to have the radar and navigation lights available when the sun goes down.

In fog, however, it would obviously be the height of stupidity not to use radar if you have it available. The fact that it is so clearly "appropriate in the prevailing circumstances and conditions" makes it compulsory.

Fortunately, as a skipper or watchleader, you don't need to decide where the boundary between optional and compulsory lies, just which side of it you are on. The simple test is whether radar – or radio, or AIS – will help you to make a fuller appraisal of the situation than you could manage without it. If the answer is "yes", then it's compulsory.

Bear in mind that if you decide not to use your radar, and are then involved in a collision, it may be quite tricky to persuade your insurance company, accident investigators, or the courts that it would not have helped you make a fuller appraisal of the situation.

Blind Arcs

Most sailing yachts have at least two significant blind arcs. Many motor boats have just one, but it's even bigger.

On most sailing yachts **1**, the biggest blind arc is created by the cabin roof (or by the dinghy and liferaft stacked on top of it) and by the spray hood. Another, rather smaller and usually overlapping, is on the lee bow, where the jib or genoa may mask almost a quarter of the horizon from anyone sitting on the windward side of the cockpit. Often, the best way to deal with this is for one person to sit on the lee side, as far aft as possible **2**. Most motor boats **3** have a huge blind arc astern, and lots of smaller ones caused by window frames and door pillars. Even a small blind arc can be dangerous if it masks a vessel which is approaching on a steady bearing, so it is important not to sit or stand in the same position for more than a few minutes at a time, and to make a point of looking astern before altering course.

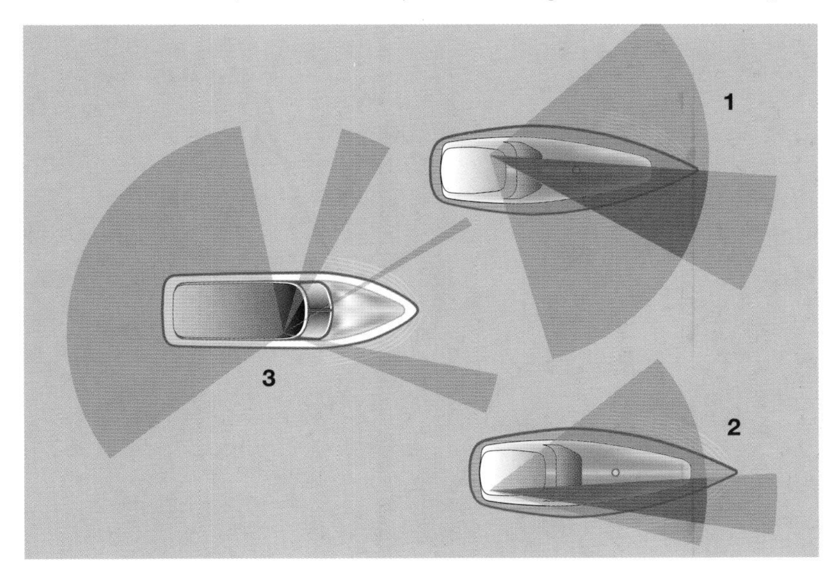

Finally, in bad weather, there is a third blind arc covering most of the windward side. Unlike the other two, it's not caused by any physical obstruction, but by the fact that it is uncomfortable or difficult to look into the wind and spray.

In an enclosed wheelhouse, rain, spray and condensation can be a major problem, particularly if your windscreen wipers or ventilators aren't up to their job. At night, internal lights reflecting from the windscreen and side windows can make it almost impossible to see out. Often the only solution is to cover the instrument panel with a cloth.

Night vision

Human beings evolved as daytime animals, but our eyes still have an amazing ability to adapt to very low levels of light – given time. But dark adaptation is a multi-stage process, and in the modern, developed world, few of us often encounter conditions that are dark enough to experience more than the first couple of stages. So after five minutes or so in "the dark", we might think that we have "got our night sight", without realising that the most significant improvements to our night vision will develop more gradually, over the next half hour or so.

Unfortunately, night vision that has taken an hour to acquire can be lost in a second if someone flashes a torch, turns on a cabin light, or strikes a match.

- Make sure everyone on board appreciates the importance of night vision and how easily it can be lost
- Use red lights, rather than white, whenever possible
- Turn instrument lights down or off, and switch big-screen instruments such as radars and chart plotters to "night mode"
- If you are short-handed, avoid the temptation to "over-navigate": preserving your night vision is probably more important than keeping a scrupulous record of the log reading or engine revs.
- On a motor boat, screen your masthead light to stop it bathing your foredeck in bright white light.

Rule 7: Risk of collision

Rule 7: Risk of collision

(a) Every vessel shall use all available means appropriate to the prevailing circumstances and conditions to determine if risk of collision exists. If there is any doubt such risk shall be deemed to exist.

(b) Proper use shall be made of radar equipment if fitted and operational, including long-range scanning to obtain early warning of risk of collision and radar plotting or equivalent systematic observation of detected objects.

(c) Assumptions shall not be made on the basis of scanty information, especially scanty radar information.

(d) In determining if risk of collision exists the following considerations shall be among those taken into account:

(i) such risk shall be deemed to exist if the compass bearing of an approaching vessel does not appreciably change;

(ii) such risk may sometimes exist even when an appreciable bearing change is evident, particularly when approaching a very large vessel or a tow or when approaching a vessel at close range.

Rules 5 and 7 use similar words to say different things.

Rule 5 is intended to make sure that you are aware of vessels which might pose a risk of collision.

Rule 7 moves on to the next stage, and deals with how to decide whether a vessel which might pose a risk of collision actually does pose a risk of collision. In particular, it warns against making rash assumptions, and describes the classic "steady bearing" test of a potential collision situation: "risk shall be deemed to exist if the compass bearing of an approaching vessel does not appreciably change".

The steady bearing test

The classic test of whether there is a risk of collision is to take a series of compass bearings of an approaching vessel. If the bearing doesn't change, you are heading for a collision or a near miss.

In practice, it's quite common to make a first assessment of risk by lining up the approaching vessel with some fixed part of the boat, such as a guardrail stanchion. If they are still lined up a few minutes later, then so long as you are on a steady course, then the bearing obviously hasn't changed.

It's important to appreciate, though, that the guardrail test is checking the relative bearing of the approaching vessel, rather than the compass bearing. Unless you are able to hold an absolutely steady course, the relative bearing may change to give a false sense of security, even when the compass bearing is constant.

Another point to bear in mind is that the compass bearing test will confirm that there is a risk of collision, but it can't be used to prove that there isn't. There are several situations in which an approaching vessel could hit you even if its compass bearing has been changing.

Two, in particular, are worth being aware of:-

- a very large vessel or long tow. If the compass bearing of the stern is reducing while the bearing of the bow is increasing (or vice versa), it means that you are likely to hit it somewhere in between!
- if either you or the other vessel are altering course or speed.

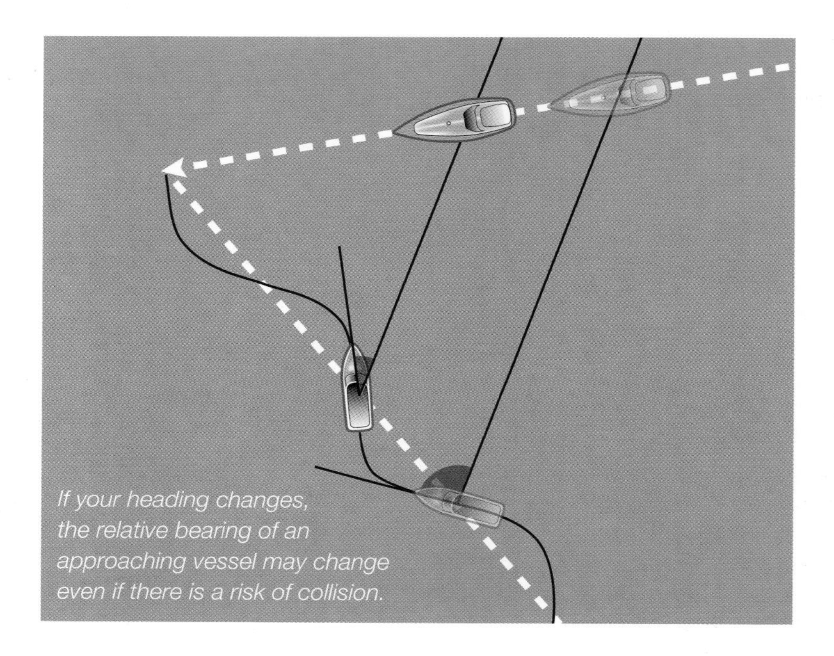
If your heading changes, the relative bearing of an approaching vessel may change even if there is a risk of collision.

Radar

Paragraph 7b is one of the most ambiguous bits in the Colregs. Is it saying:-
"Proper use shall be made of ***radar****"*
or
*"**Proper** use shall be made of radar"?*

Different authorities have taken different views on this: the US Coast Guard, for instance, seem to favour the first interpretation ("If you have radar you must use it"), while the British MCA incline the other way, and say that it means "if you use radar, you must use it properly" – that it must be set up for optimum performance and on a suitable range scale.

What they do agree on is that proper use of radar involves more than glancing at the screen every now and again. At the very least, the position of each blob on the screen needs to be monitored, either by a human observer or by some kind of automatic radar plotting device (such as MARPA, ARPA, ATA , or ARP) to see whether any of them appear to be moving straight towards the centre.

Rule 6: Safe speed

Rule 6: Safe speed

Every vessel shall at all times proceed at a safe speed so that she can take proper and effective action to avoid collision and be stopped within a distance appropriate to the prevailing circumstances and conditions. In determining a safe speed the following factors shall be among those taken into account:

(a) By all vessels:
- (i) the state of visibility;
- (ii) the traffic density including concentrations of fishing vessels or any other vessels;
- (iii) the manoeuvrability of the vessel with special reference to stopping distance and turning ability in the prevailing conditions;
- (iv) at night the presence of background light such as from shore lights or from back scatter of her own lights;
- (v) the state of wind, sea and current, and the proximity of navigational hazards;
- (vi) the draught in relation to the available depth of water.

(b) Additionally, by vessels with operational radar:
- (i) the characteristics, efficiency and limitations of the radar equipment;
- (ii) any constraints imposed by the radar range scale in use;
- (iii) the effect on radar detection of the sea state, weather and other sources of interference;
- (iv) the possibility that small vessels, ice and other floating objects may not be detected by radar at an adequate range;
- (v) the number, location and movement of vessels detected by radar;
- vi) the more exact assessment of the visibility that may be possible when radar is used to determine the range of vessels or other objects in the vicinity.

Speed, alone, seldom causes collisions, but it increases stopping distances and turning circles, reduces thinking time and – when a collision does happen – increases the amount of damage done. It is hardly surprising, then, that speed is identified as a contributory factor in something like 60% of collisions that are formally investigated.

Rather than setting an arbitrary one-size-fits-all speed limit, the Colregs set out a number of factors that should be taken into account when deciding on a "safe speed". For the most part, these are a check-list of common-sense precautions: you hardly need to consult the rule book to appreciate that driving a boat at high speed through crowded waters at night and with a background of shore lights to confuse matters is potentially dangerous.

Unfortunately, it is not just small vessels that operate at dangerously high speed. Accident investigators looking into the collision between the 14-metre *Wahkuna* and the 277 metre container ship *Nedlloyd Vespucci* found that the container ship was doing 25 knots through visibility that was reported to be as little as fifty metres. And she wasn't the only one: coastal radar surveillance of the area showed that out of nineteen other ships in the vicinity, only one had reduced speed because of the conditions.

Faced with such wholesale disregard for the rules, small craft have one very powerful defence: we are generally very manoeuvrable. But sailing yachtsmen, in particular, need to take care not to jeopardise that manoeuvrability by setting unnecessarily complicated rigs or by letting their speed fall so low that they cannot get out of the way of an approaching ship.

To take an extreme example, a ketch, broad-reaching under mizzen staysail and spinnaker and with preventers on the main and mizzen booms might well take ten minutes or more to alter course – during which a container ship like Nedlloyd Vespucci *would have travelled four miles.*

3: Who gives way?

Rules that apply when another vessel is in sight

The second section of the steering and sailing rules is sub-titled "Conduct of vessels in sight of one another", and it includes several rules that have survived essentially unchanged since 1863.

Rule 11: Application

Rule 11: Application
Rules in this Section apply to vessels in sight of one another.

Rule 11 applies to:-
Rule 12: Sailing vessels (see page 24)
Rule 13: Overtaking (see page 16)
Rule 14: Head on situation (see page 22)
Rule 15: Crossing situation (see page 21)
Rule 16: Action by give-way vessel (see page 26)
Rule 17: Action by stand-on vessel (see page 28)
and Rule 18: Responsibilities between vessels (see page 19)

The point of this apparently fatuous rule is to make it quite clear that these rules do not apply when two vessels can detect each other only by hearing or by radar.

Rule 13: Overtaking
and Rule 18: Responsibilities between vessels

These two rules, between them, set out a clear "pecking order".

In open water, you must keep out of the way of anyone that is higher in the pecking order than you:

- a vessel which you are overtaking
- a vessel not under command
- a vessel restricted in its ability to manoeuvre
- a vessel constrained by its draught
- a vessel engaged in fishing
- a sailing vessel
- a power-driven vessel
- a seaplane or WIG craft (wing in ground-effect)

Rule 13: Overtaking

(a) Notwithstanding anything contained in the Rules of Part B, Sections I and II, any vessel overtaking any other shall keep out of the way of the vessel being overtaken.

(b) A vessel shall be deemed to be overtaking when coming up with another vessel from a direction more than 22.5 degrees abaft her beam, that is, in such a position with reference to the vessel she is overtaking, that at night she would be able to see only the stern light of that vessel but neither of her sidelights.

(c) When a vessel is in any doubt as to whether she is overtaking another, she shall assume that this is the case and act accordingly.

(d) Any subsequent alteration of the bearing between the two vessels shall not make the overtaking vessel a crossing vessel within the meaning of these Rules or relieve her of the duty of keeping clear of the overtaken vessel until she is finally past and clear.

Overtaking
It is impossible to overstate the significance of the first dozen words of this rule, which set out its clear and absolute priority over all the other "steering and sailing" rules apart from Rule 19.

So far as the skippers of small craft are concerned, it means that a fast-moving sailing vessel may well be required to give way to a slow-moving motor boat – particularly in and around harbours, where powered craft are often subject to speed limits that sailors may not even know about.

The idea that the vessel which is overtaking has to keep clear is simple and familiar: it's just the same on the road. Ships and boats, however, are not confined to narrow ribbons of tarmac, so at sea, you are regarded as "overtaking" if you are approaching another vessel from anywhere within an arc of 67.5° either side of dead astern.

Of course, as the overtaker pulls ahead, the relative bearing between the two vessels is bound to change, but paragraph (d) makes it clear that this doesn't alter their relative status: the overtaking vessel is still obliged to keep clear of the other until she is "finally past and clear".

This obligation does not give the vessel that is being overtaken the right to alter course into the path of the overtaker. Rule 17 (see page 28) imposes important responsibilities on the "stand-on" vessel, of which the most important is to maintain her course and speed.

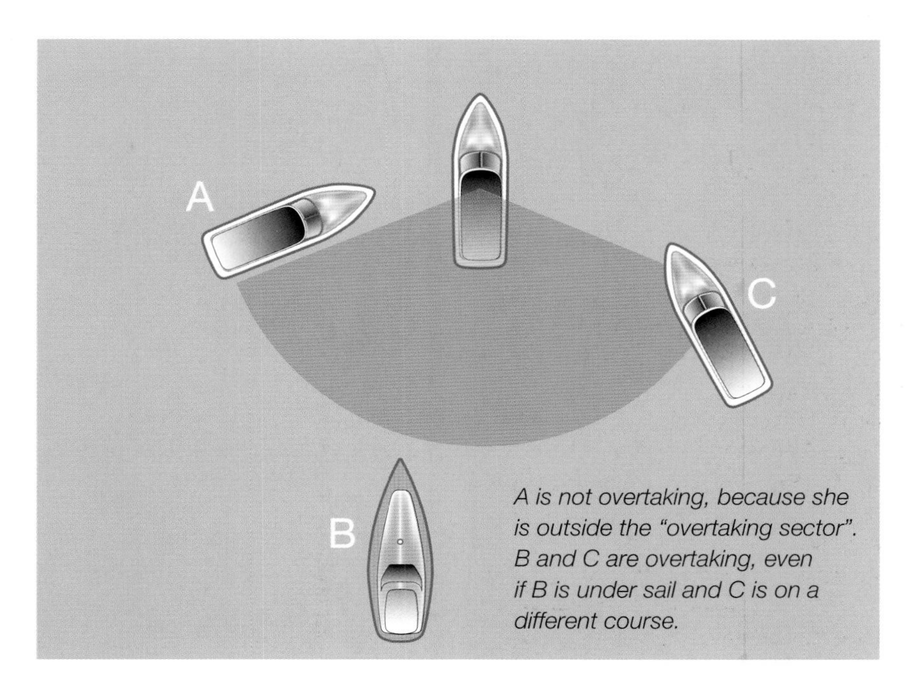

A is not overtaking, because she is outside the "overtaking sector". B and C are overtaking, even if B is under sail and C is on a different course.

This makes it important to get into the habit of looking astern before altering course.

Motorcyclists call this quick look over the shoulder the "lifesaver". It is just as useful at sea.

A changing situation

The situation shown in fig 1. in which it appears that the overtaking vessel has ignored Rule 13: she was the overtaking vessel at first (B) but then, as she drew alongside the slower vessel (A), she altered course to port – presumably intending to pass ahead.

But suppose we had only seen the latter stages of the manoeuvre? In that case, as in the smaller diagram, there's no reason to assume that (B) was overtaking. Instead, she appears to be a "crossing vessel", and (A) is the one that has to give way (see page 26).

In spite of the Rule 13d, the fact that you may once have strayed into someone's overtaking arc does not mean that you are bound to give way to them to the end of time!

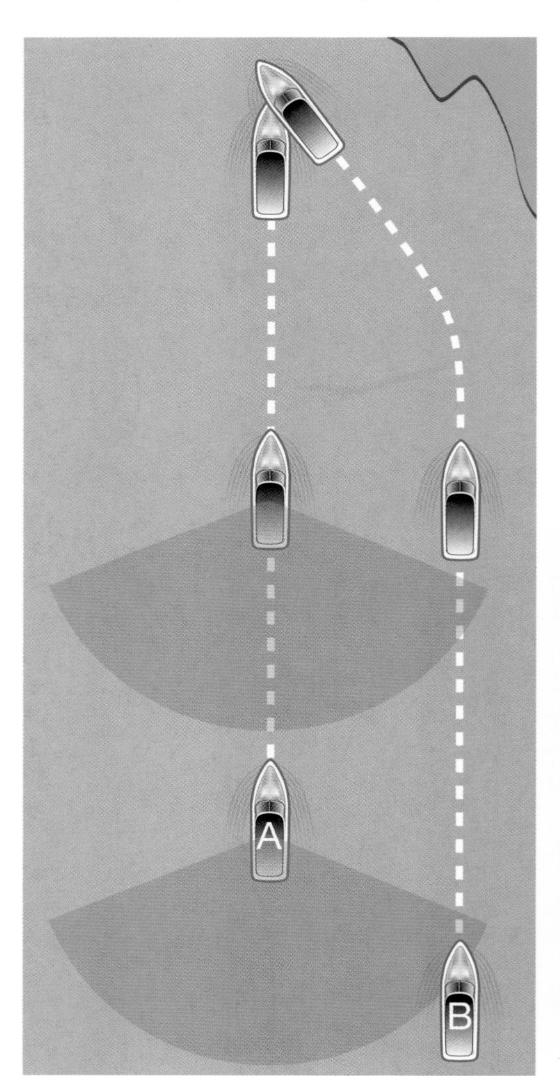

fig 1

The key factor is when the change from "overtaking" to "crossing" takes place, and how far apart the two vessels are at the time.

Various court cases seem to suggest that if the change from overtaking to crossing takes place while the vessels are two or three miles apart, it should be regarded as a crossing situation, rather than as overtaking.

These legal precedents, however, concern ships, rather than small craft. For smaller or more manoeuvrable vessels the critical distance could be well under a mile, and might even reduce to a few boat lengths.

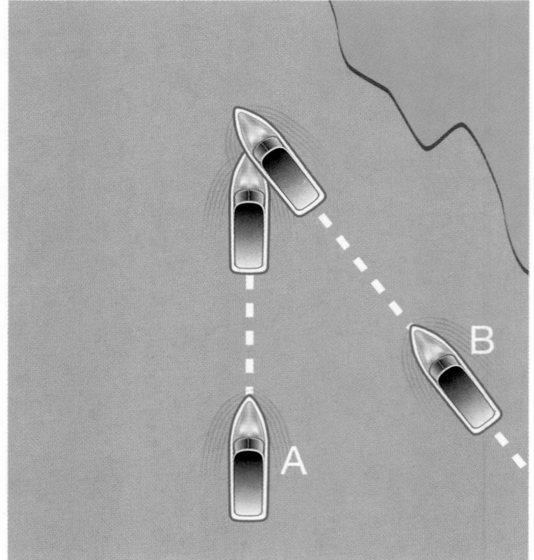

fig 2

Interaction

It is never enough to "just miss" another vessel. Rule 8 (see page 26) specifies that any action taken to avoid collision should result in the vessels passing "at a safe distance".

This is particularly true when a large vessel is overtaking or being overtaken by a much smaller one, because it is under these circumstances that interaction – caused by pressure waves around their hulls – is likely to occur.

> *After the fatal collision between the dredger* Bowbelle *and the disco boat* Marchioness, *the Marine Accident Investigation Branch report said "... when a relatively large ship is overtaking a smaller one, the latter will tend to sheer across the bow of the former. Where the two vessels are very close, the effect can be so great that the smaller vessel loses all control. It is highly likely that this effect was a cause, probably the major cause, of* Marchioness *sheering across the bow of* Bowbelle*".*

A much less subtle kind of interaction almost certainly accounted for the loss of the sailing yacht *Ouzo* and her three crew, after what was widely reported as a collision with the ferry *Pride of Bilbao*. The formal report, however, suggests that it was probably a very near miss, rather than a collision, and that *Ouzo* was swamped or capsized by the ferry's wash.

Rule 18: Responsibilities between vessels

Except where Rules 9, 10 and 13 otherwise require:

(a) A power-driven vessel underway shall keep out of the way of:
- (i) a vessel not under command;
- (ii) a vessel restricted in her ability to manoeuvre;
- (iii) a vessel engaged in fishing;
- (iv) a sailing vessel.

(b) A sailing vessel underway shall keep out of the way of:
- (i) a vessel not under command;
- (ii) a vessel restricted in her ability to manoeuvre;
- (iii) a vessel engaged in fishing.

(c) A vessel engaged in fishing when underway shall, so far as possible, keep out of the way of:
- (i) a vessel not under command;
- (ii) a vessel restricted in her ability to manoeuvre.

(d)
- (i) Any vessel other than a vessel not under command or a vessel restricted in her ability to manoeuvre shall, if the circumstances of the case admit, avoid impeding the safe passage of a vessel constrained by her draught, exhibiting the signals in Rule 28.
- (ii) A vessel constrained by her draught shall navigate with particular caution having full regard to her special condition.

(e) A seaplane on the water shall, in general, keep well clear of all vessels and avoid impeding their navigation. In circumstances, however, where risk of collision exists, she shall comply with the Rules of this Part.

(f)
- (i) A WIG craft shall, when taking off, landing and in flight near the surface, keep well clear of all other vessels and avoid impeding their navigation;
- (ii) A WIG craft operating on the water surface shall comply with the Rules of this Part as a power-driven vessel.

Rule 18: Hampered vessels

Rule 18 sets out several categories of vessel that may be less able to manoeuvre than normal power driven vessels, and which therefore deserve special treatment.

A seaplane or WIG craft is pretty unmistakable, but some of the other types of hampered vessels are much less easy to identify. For this reason, Rules 25-28 specify various lights and day signals to be shown by vessels that are claiming special status. Rules 25-28 are covered in more detail on pages 52-58, but they are summarised in the table below:

	Rule 3 definition	Day Signal	Lights
Not under command	A vessel which through some exceptional circumstance is unable to manoeuvre as required by these Rules and is therefore unable to keep out of the way of another vessel.		
Restricted in ability to manoeuvre	A vessel which from the nature of her work is restricted in her ability to manoeuvre as required by these Rules and is therefore unable to keep out of the way of another vessel.		
Constrained by draught	A power-driven vessel which, because of her draught in relation to the available depth and width of navigable water, is severely restricted in her ability to deviate from the course she is following.		
Engaged in fishing (note light illustration shows two different light signals. Green and white is 'Trawling'; red and white is 'Fishing other than Trawling'.)	Any vessel fishing with nets, lines, trawls or other fishing apparatus which restrict manoeuvrability, but does not include a vessel fishing with trolling lines or other fishing apparatus which do not restrict manoeuvrability.		
Sailing vessel	Any vessel under sail provided that propelling machinery, if fitted, is not being used.		
As a power vessel	A vessel proceeding under sail when also being propelled by machinery.		

Rules 14 and 15: Power meets power

Most motor boaters will never come across a vessel that is not under command, and quite a few will go a lifetime without coming across one that is constrained by its draught or restricted in its ability to manoeuvre. For most of us, the vast majority of our potential collisions are with other power-driven vessels, on the same rung of the pecking order as ourselves. And apart from overtaking situations (see page 16), there are only two ways that power-driven vessels can collide with each other: head on, or crossing.

Rule 15: Crossing situation

When two power-driven vessels are crossing so as to involve risk of collision, the vessel which has the other on her own starboard side shall keep out of the way and shall, if the circumstances of the case admit, avoid crossing ahead of the other vessel.

Rule 15 is a short and simple rule that says *"the vessel which has the other on her own starboard side shall keep out of the way"*. In this respect, it is exactly the same as the rule that applies on British roads when two vehicles meet at a mini roundabout.

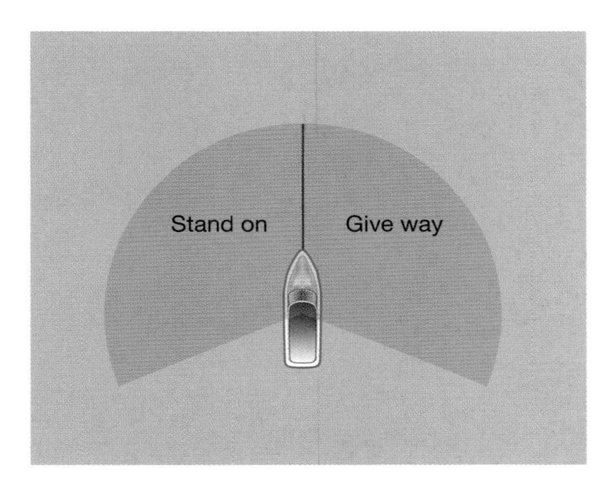

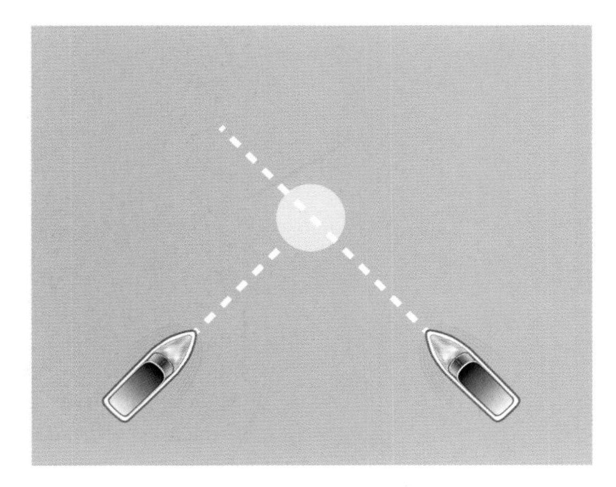

The second part of the rule says that the give-way vessel *"shall, if the circumstances of the case admit, avoid crossing ahead of the other vessel"*.

When you are required to give way to a vessel that is crossing from your right hand side, there are two ways to avoid crossing ahead of it:-

- alter course to starboard
- slow down

Only in the most unusual circumstances is there any justification for altering course to port.

Rule 14: Head-on situation

(a) When two power-driven vessels are meeting on reciprocal or nearly reciprocal courses so as to involve risk of collision each shall alter her course to starboard so that each shall pass on the port side of the other.

(b) Such a situation shall be deemed to exist when a vessel sees the other ahead or nearly ahead and by night she would see the mast head lights of the other in a line or nearly in a line and/or both sidelights and by day she observes the corresponding aspect of the other vessel.

(c) When a vessel is in any doubt as to whether such a situation exists she shall assume that it does exist and act accordingly.

Rule 14 is slightly longer than Rule 15, but it looks even simpler. There is no need to work out who gives way and who stands on, because both vessels are required to alter course to starboard.

But away from the hypothetical world in which all vessels steer absolutely steady courses, move in constant straight lines and have perfectly aligned lights, it is not always easy to tell whether a vessel really is "ahead or nearly ahead" or not, or whether it really is on a reciprocal course.

There are three possibilities to consider:

- that there really is a serious risk of collision
- that the two vessels are heading for a near miss in which they will pass close down each other's port sides
- that the two vessels are heading for a near miss in which they will pass close down each other's starboard sides

In the first case (fig 1), in which there really is a risk of collision, the risk can be eliminated if both vessels obey the rule, and both alter course to starboard.

Even if the watchkeeper on one vessel misinterprets the situation, and does nothing, the risk of collision will be significantly reduced or eliminated if the other vessel alters course to starboard.

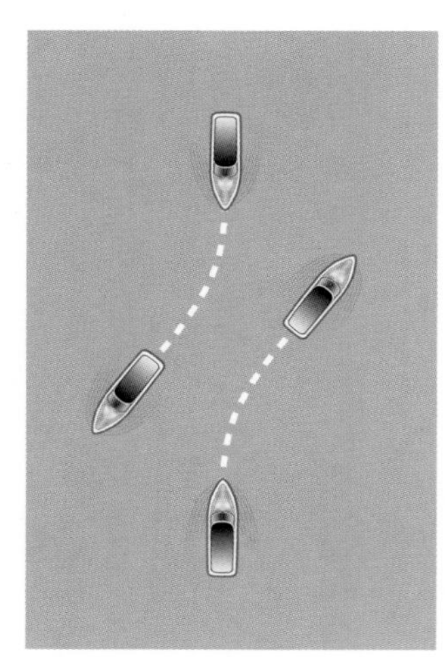

fig 1

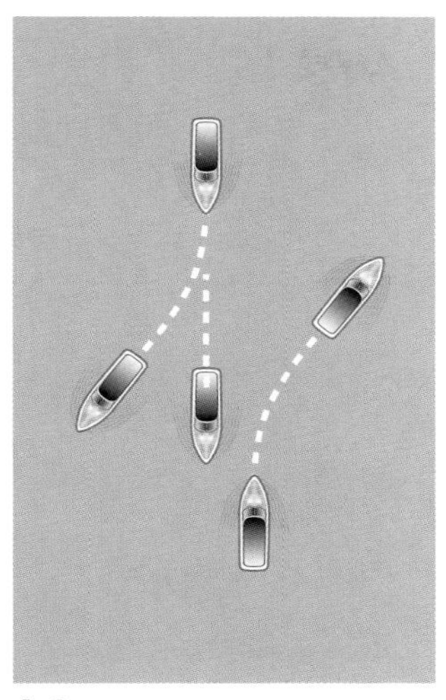
fig 2

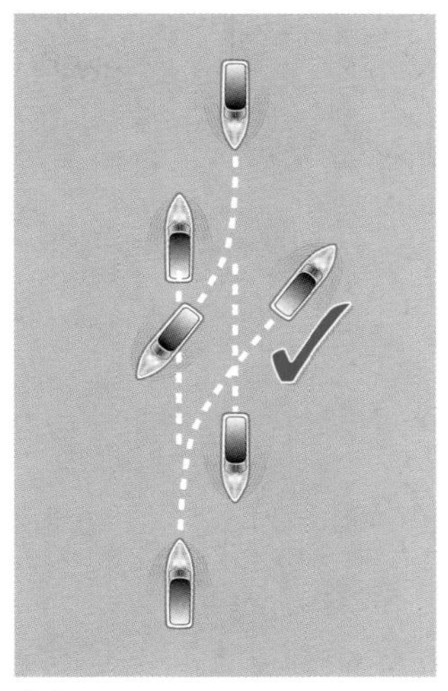
fig 3

In the second case (fig 2), in which a near miss looks more likely than an actual collision, there is no harm done if either or both of the vessels alters course to starboard: it will simply increase the distance between them.

The third situation (fig 3) is the dangerous one, because one watchkeeper might well think "this is a head-on situation, in which the rules require me to alter course to starboard" while his opposite number on the other vessel thinks "if I alter course to port, it will widen the gap between us."

But by doing so, they will have converted a near miss into a potential collision. The golden rule is **do not alter course to port**.

If the situation is so close that you are tempted to "widen the gap" by altering course to port, then it is obviously so close that you think there is a risk of collision (If there is no risk, then why are you thinking about widening the gap?). And if there is a risk of collision, then the last paragraph of the Rule applies, and tells you to alter course to starboard.

If you are ever faced with someone who has altered course to port when you have altered to starboard, you have a very real problem. You don't know whether the person in charge of the other vessel will realise his mistake, and try to correct it by turning back to starboard, or whether he will compound it by turning further to port. The only safe options are to stop or – if there is time – to continue your turn through 180°, and run away.

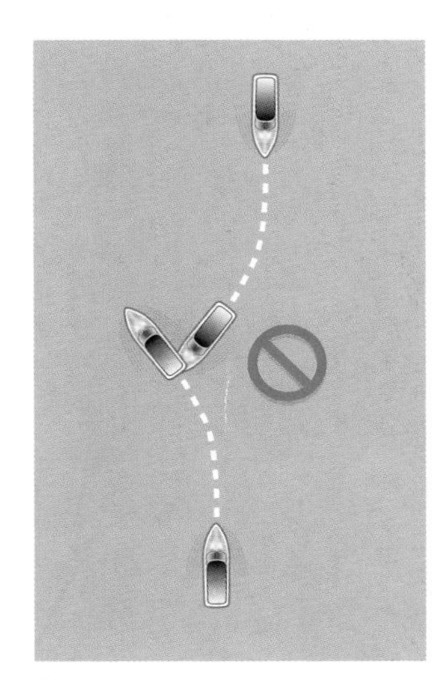
fig 4

Rule 12: Sail meets sail

The Colregs that apply when two sailing vessels meet are very similar to the corresponding racing rules, but there are differences, so racing sailors still need to remember that the racing rules only apply to boats that are also racing. If a boat that is racing meets a boat that just happens to be in the vicinity, then the collision regulations apply, rather than the racing rules.

The main difference – apart from the absence of rules about starting, finishing, rounding marks and being entitled to "room" – is that Colreg Rule 13 (the overtaking rule) applies just as much to sailing boats as to anyone else.

Rule 12: Sailing Vessels

(a) When two sailing vessels are approaching one another, so as to involve risk of collision, one of them shall keep out of the way of the other as follows:

- (i) when each has the wind on a different side, the vessel which has the wind on the port side shall keep out of the way of the other;
- (ii) when both have the wind on the same side, the vessel which is to windward shall keep out of the way of the vessel which is to leeward;
- (iii) if a vessel with the wind on the port side sees a vessel to windward and cannot determine with certainty whether the other vessel has the wind on the port or on the starboard side, she shall keep out of the way of the other.

(b) For the purposes of this Rule the windward side shall be deemed to be the side opposite to that on which the mainsail is carried or, in the case of a square-rigged vessel, the side opposite to that on which the largest fore-and-aft sail is carried.

Paragraph a(i) is effectively the same as Rule 10 of the racing rules, which says: *"When boats are on opposite tacks, a port-tack boat shall keep clear of a starboard-tack boat."*

Paragraph a(ii) is similar to Rule 11 of the racing rules, which says *"When boats are on the same tack ... a windward boat shall keep clear of a leeward boat."*

These two paragraphs are very simple and clear-cut. There is one particular situation, however, in which they don't work. That special case is dealt with by paragraph a(iii) which handles situations in which it is impossible to be sure whether the approaching vessel is on port or starboard tack.

- If the other vessel is to leeward of you, then there is unlikely to be any doubt about which tack it is on.
- If you are on starboard tack, then there can be no doubt that the onus is on the other vessel to give way, because one or the other of the two earlier sections of the rule must apply.

So this part of the rule only applies if the other vessel is to windward of you **and** you are on port tack – i.e. with the wind blowing onto the port side of the boat, or with the mainsail on the starboard side. It says, in effect, that if you don't know whether you are the give way vessel or not, then you should assume that you are.

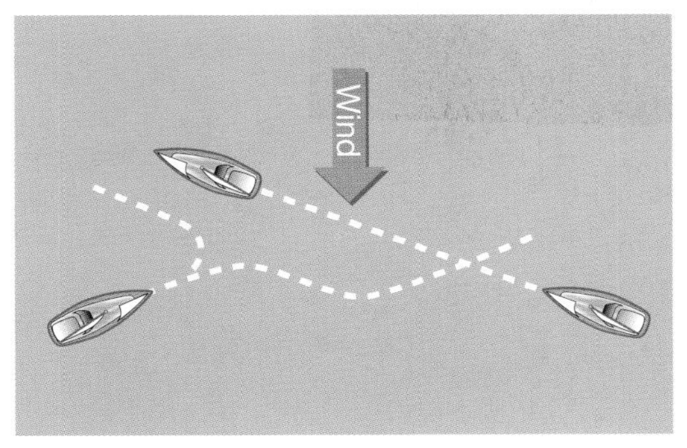

fig 1

A sailing vessel with the wind on her port side must keep out of the way of one with the wind on her starboard side.

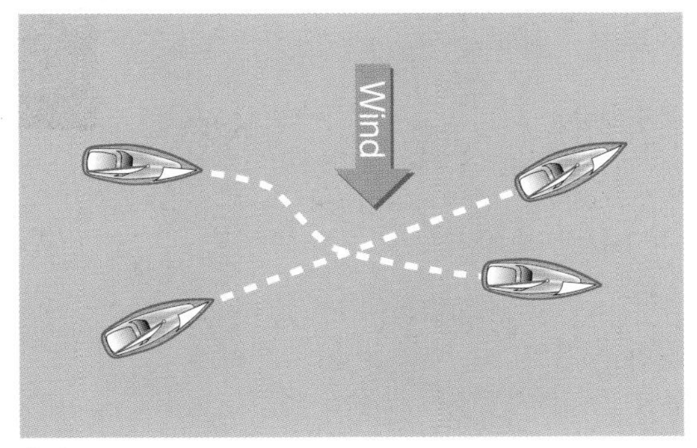

fig 2

A sailing vessel which is to windward of another must keep out of the way of the other.

Faced with this situation, it's worth bearing in mind that although **you** don't know which tack the other vessel is on, **her** watchkeeper does. So what appears to you to be an ambiguous situation should seem perfectly clear-cut to him.

- If he is on starboard tack, he will be expecting you to give way under Rule 12(a)(i) – so the fact that you have done so by applying Rule 12(a)(iii) won't make any difference to him: he should hold his course and speed (see page 28) and let you manoeuvre round him.
- If he is on port tack, then he will believe himself to be the give way vessel under Rule 12(a)(ii). He may well want to avoid gybeing, and will almost certainly want to avoid passing ahead of you, so he is most likely to luff up.

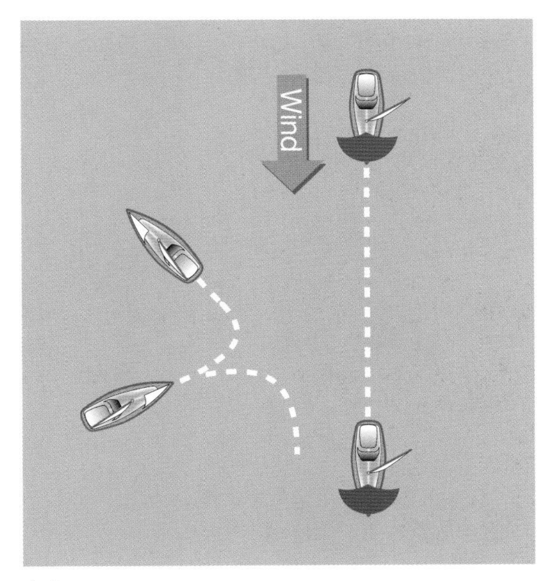

fig 3

If in doubt, a port tack vessel should give way.

This means that if you want to take evasive action by tacking, it is particularly important to do it very early. If you have left it late, or if there is any doubt in your mind, the safest course of action is to bear away onto a parallel course, and then reappraise the situation.

4: Giving way and standing on

Rules that apply when another vessel is in sight

In the language of the collision regulations, there are "Give-Way" vessels, and there are "Stand-On" vessels. There is no such thing as a "Right of Way".

The responsibilities of a Give-Way vessel are set out in considerable detail in Rule 8, and are summarised rather neatly in the single sentence of Rule 16, while those of the Stand-On vessel are given in Rule 17.

There is a subtle significance in the fact that the Give-Way and Stand-On rules are so far apart.
- Rule 8 is in Part B Section 1, whose rules deal with the conduct of vessels in any condition of visibility.
- Rule 17 is in Part B Section 2, where the rules are concerned only with vessels that are in sight of each other.

Rules 16 and 8: Giving Way

Rule 16: Action by give-way vessel
Every vessel which is directed to keep out of the way of another vessel shall, so far as possible, take early and substantial action to keep well clear.

Rule 8: Action to avoid collision
(a) Any action taken to avoid collision shall be taken in accordance with the Rules of this Part and shall, if the circumstances of the case admit, be positive, made in ample time and with due regard to the observance of good seamanship.
(b) Any alteration of course and/or speed to avoid collision shall, if the circumstances of the case admit, be large enough to be readily apparent to another vessel observing visually or by radar; a succession of small alterations of course and/or speed should be avoided.
(c) If there is sufficient sea-room, alteration of course alone may be the most effective action to avoid a close-quarters situation provided that it is made in good time, is substantial and does not result in another close-quarters situation.
(d) Action taken to avoid collision with another vessel shall be such as to result in passing at a safe distance. The effectiveness of the action shall be carefully checked until the other vessel is finally past and clear.
(e) If necessary to avoid collision or allow more time to assess the situation, a vessel shall slacken her speed or take all way off by stopping or reversing her means of propulsion.
(f)
  (i) A vessel which, by any of these Rules, is required not to impede the passage or safe passage of another vessel shall, when required by the circumstances of the case, take early action to allow sufficient sea-room for the safe passage of the other vessel.
  (ii) A vessel required not to impede the passage or safe passage of another vessel is not relieved of this obligation if approaching the other vessel so as to involve risk of collision and shall, when taking action, have full regard to the action which may be required by the Rules of this Part.
  (iii) A vessel the passage of which is not to be impeded remains fully obliged to comply with the Rules of this Part when the two vessels are approaching one another so as to involve risk of collision.

Rule 8 is probably one of the most complicated and contentious rules in the book, but the tricky bits are all in paragraph (a). The first five shorter paragraphs are much more straightforward.

Positive, referring to an alteration of course, means one that is large enough to be obvious to the watchkeeper on the other vessel. In other words, it should be enough to make your vessel look significantly different. How large an alteration of course is required to achieve this will vary depending on the circumstances. If you are meeting another vessel almost head on at night, altering course by ten degrees may be enough to show the other vessel a red side light instead of a green one (see page 45). But if the other vessel is looking at your side, rather than at your bow, an alteration of as much as thirty or forty degrees may be imperceptible: to make yourself look radically different, you need to turn so that you are aiming straight towards him.

Ample time does not mean "as soon as you see him". If you are proceeding at a safe speed and keeping a proper lookout, there should be plenty of time to make a proper assessment of the situation before rushing into avoiding action. What it does mean is that the other vessel's watchkeeper should never feel any doubt about whether you are going to be taking avoiding action, or not.

Unfortunately, this isn't much help, because the other watchkeeper's feelings may depend on many factors, including the weather conditions, the amount of sea room available, the size and manoeuvrability of his vessel, and his own experience – both in general and in previous encounters with vessels like yours. When dealing with a ship in open water and good visibility, a good rule of thumb for a small boat skipper is that you should alter course by the time you can see the ship's waterline.

In confined waters, Southampton's "moving exclusion zone" extending 1000 metres ahead and 100 metres on each side of a ship gives a very good idea of what ship masters and pilots are likely to regard as "uncomfortably close", but remember that you need to alter course to stay out of the "exclusion zone" well before you get into it.

Estimating Range

Estimating the range of a large vessel is always difficult. It is useful to remember that the distance to the horizon (in miles) is approximately twice the square root of your height of eye in metres. So for most recreational craft, the horizon is between about two and five miles away. If you can see the ship's actual waterline, her range is less than the distance to the horizon.

Rule 17: Standing on

Rule 17: Action by stand-on vessel

(a) (i) Where one of two vessels is to keep out of the way the other shall keep her course and speed.

(ii) The latter vessel may however take action to avoid collision by her manoeuvre alone, as soon as it becomes apparent to her that the vessel required to keep out of the way is not taking appropriate action in compliance with these Rules.

(b) When, from any cause, the vessel required to keep her course and speed finds herself so close that collision cannot be avoided by the action of the give-way vessel alone, she shall take such action as will best aid to avoid collision.

(c) A power-driven vessel which takes action in a crossing situation in accordance with sub-paragraph (a)(ii) of this Rule to avoid collision with another power-driven vessel shall, if the circumstances of the case admit, not alter course to port for a vessel on her own port side.

(d) This Rule does not relieve the give-way vessel of her obligation to keep out of the way.

The primary responsibility of a stand-on vessel is spelt out in words of one syllable in the first sentence of the first paragraph: she "...**shall** keep her course and speed".

The word "shall" makes it mandatory: holding your course and speed is not a "right" that you are able to relinquish at will, but a responsibility.

But – and this is what makes the stand-on vessel's responsibility more onerous than that of the give-way vessel – the requirement to hold her course and speed does not mean that she is obliged to plough on regardless, from when a distant vessel first appears over the horizon until the moment of impact. Nor is she required to run herself aground or into a collision with some other vessel!

So far as the stand-on vessel is concerned, a developing collision situation could be said to consist of four distinct phases.

The preliminary phase – no perceptible risk of collision

The preliminary phase is when two vessels are out of sight of each other, or are so far apart that there is no real risk of collision. In a court case at the end of the nineteenth century, the judge decided that *"... nobody could seriously contend that if two ships are six miles apart, the Regulations for Preventing Collisions apply to them"*.

Both vessels, at this stage, are perfectly entitled to go about their normal business, even if this means altering course and speed.

That legal precedent still stands, even though times have moved on, and for two large, fast ships, six miles is now well within the distance at which their watchkeepers should be eyeing each other somewhat warily.

The first phase – compulsory stand on

At some point, however, the watchkeeper on one of the vessels decides that there is a risk of collision, and that he is the stand-on vessel. At that moment, the collision rules kick in... and at this stage, he has no reason to believe that his counterpart on the give-way vessel will do anything other than follow them correctly.

His task at this stage is to stand on, keeping his course and speed, but monitoring the developing situation.

That simple directive to "keep her course and speed", has been part of the Colregs for long enough to have been the subject of numerous legal arguments, and it is now more than a century since a court decided that it did not actually mean "keep going in a straight line and at a constant speed". Back in 1908, it was decided that a stand-on vessel was perfectly entitled to continue with the "ordinary and proper manoeuvre in the course of navigation" of stopping to pick up a pilot.

For sailors, manoeuvres such as tacking and gybing are much more "ordinary and proper" than stopping to pick up a pilot, but it is unlikely that the courts would agree with anyone who used this as an excuse for tacking across the bows of an approaching ship – even if you were alive to plead your case.

The 1908 judgement reasoned that the test of whether a manoeuvre by a stand-on vessel was acceptable was whether it was "an ordinary and proper manoeuvre in the course of navigation" and "ought the other vessel to be aware of the manoeuvre which is being attempted to be carried out?"

The second phase – optional action

In practice, most potential collision situations are resolved before they get as far as phase two, which begins when the stand-on watchkeeper realises that the give-way vessel is not, in fact giving way. For ship-on-ship encounters in open water, this is likely to be when the two vessels are two or three miles apart, but in confined waters, or for small or very manoeuvrable vessels, it may be considerably less.

This is the point at which many ships' watchkeepers reach for the whistle or the VHF, and start trying to contact the other vessel.

It is also the point at which the stand-on vessel's obligation to hold its course and speed ends: at any point from now on her watchkeeper has the option of taking action.

Even at this late stage, it is quite possible that the give-way vessel may still take avoiding action, probably by turning to starboard. This means that the best avoiding action by the stand-on vessel is usually a bold turn to starboard.

Paragraph (c) makes the turn to starboard almost compulsory, but not quite. It leaves the option of turning to port available for sailing vessels and for those claiming special status (such as restricted in ability to manoeuvre). Even for those that are allowed to turn to port, however, turning to starboard may still be the better move.

Communications in collision avoidance

The US Coast Guard encourages ships to make radio contact with each other to resolve potential collisions, but they are out on a bit of a limb: almost every other government – including the UK – disapproves of VHF radio being used for collision avoidance, and would rather we simply followed the rules!

Sound signals, on the other hand, are compulsory, under Rule 34d (see page 61).

The third phase – compulsory action

The third and final stage of the situation begins when "collision **cannot** be avoided by the action of the give-way vessel alone".

Most vessels have a turning circle of about four ship-lengths, so if the give-way vessel happens to be one of the world's largest ships, this stage could begin when the two vessels are still almost a mile apart. For two small craft, on the other hand, it may be a matter of a few tens of metres.

At this point, two things happen:-

- avoiding action ceases to be an option, and becomes compulsory, and
- turning to port becomes an acceptable and legitimate manoeuvre.

In the nastiest kind of potential collision – between a small craft and a large ship – this third phase typically begins when the two vessels are a few hundred metres apart. At that stage, the ship has run out of options, but the smaller vessel still has plenty of time and distance in which to stop or turn round.

The best bet is to turn onto an almost reciprocal course to the ship, so as to meet its head and stern waves head-on.

How close?

The very highly respected professional textbook "A Guide to the Collision Regulations" suggests that "in the open sea it is suggested that a stand-on vessel should not allow a give-way vessel to approach to a distance of less than about twelve times her own length in a crossing situation without taking avoiding action".

This is not strictly logical, because the point at which action by the stand-on vessel becomes compulsory depends on the manoeuvrability of the give-way vessel, so it cannot possibly be linked to the length of the stand-on vessel. But it is a good indication of what is regarded as "best practice" amongst those who earn their livings at sea.

Handling characteristics of ships

Ships are often moving much faster than they appear to be. Typical service speeds are for tankers 10-15 knots, container ships 20-26 knots and passenger liners/large ferries 20-30 knots. They are not, however, quite as unmanoeuvrable as many people believe. Even a large tanker can be "crash stopped" in about 1.5 miles, though they tend to avoid doing it. Most watchkeepers are more likely to give way by altering course.

The diameter of a typical turning circle is about 4-5 times the ship's length, and takes about 5-10 minutes to complete. But altering course by 10 degrees is very much quicker. Altering course by 10 degrees at a range of six miles is generally enough to convert a collision into a 1-mile miss.

5: Narrow channels and separation schemes

Rules that always apply

Rules 9 and 10 deal with narrow channels and traffic separation schemes.

Narrow channels, in general, are close inshore – often, but not always, in the approaches to natural harbours. Traffic separation schemes, by contrast, are entirely man-made: they are lines drawn on charts, usually with no physical boundaries in the real world, that are set up to keep ships apart in what most small craft navigators would regard as "open water".

Despite the contrasts between narrow channels and traffic separation schemes, there are distinct similarities between them, including the appearance of the most ambiguous expression in the collision regulations: a requirement that vessels less than 20m in length "shall not impede" a vessel that is confined to the channel or separation scheme.

Rule 9: Narrow channels

Rule 9: Narrow channels

(a) A vessel proceeding along the course of a narrow channel or fairway shall keep as near to the outer limit of the channel or fairway which lies on her starboard side as is safe and practicable.

(b) A vessel of less than 20 metres in length or a sailing vessel shall not impede the passage of a vessel which can safely navigate only within a narrow channel or fairway.

(c) A vessel engaged in fishing shall not impede the passage of any other vessel navigating within a narrow channel or fairway.

(d) A vessel shall not cross a narrow channel or fairway if such crossing impedes the passage of a vessel which can safely navigate only within such channel or fairway. The latter vessel may use the sound signal prescribed in Rule 34(d) if in doubt as to the intention of the crossing vessel.

(e) (i) In a narrow channel or fairway when overtaking can take place only if the vessel to be overtaken has to take action to permit safe passing, the vessel intending to overtake shall indicate her intention by sounding the appropriate signal prescribed in Rule 34(c)(i). The vessel to be overtaken shall, if in agreement, sound the appropriate signal prescribed in Rule 34(c)(ii) and take steps to permit safe passing. If in doubt she may sound the signals prescribed in Rule 34(d).

(ii) This Rule does not relieve the overtaking vessel of her obligation under Rule 13.

(f) A vessel nearing a bend or an area of a narrow channel or fairway where other vessels may be obscured by an intervening obstruction shall navigate with particular alertness and caution and shall sound the appropriate signal prescribed in Rule 34(e).

(g) Any vessel shall, if the circumstances of the case admit, avoid anchoring in a narrow channel.

Rule 9: Narrow channels cont'd

The principles behind the rule are quite simple, and boil down to:-

(a) drive on the right
(b) small craft, don't obstruct the channel
(c) small craft, don't obstruct the channel, even if you are fishing
(d) don't cross the channel in front of vessels going along it
(e) use sound signals
(f) be careful at blind bends
(g) don't anchor in the channel

What is narrow?

Although this rule refers specifically to "narrow channels", the meaning of "narrow" is not defined. It is easy to see why: what constitutes a "narrow channel" to the captain of a 250,000 ton tanker could very well be open water to a 25 ton motor cruiser – and crossing it could be quite an adventure for the paddler of a 25 kilo canoe!

But Rule 9 is not a "might is right" rule: it does not give ships the right to claim the whole of the Irish Sea or English Channel as "a narrow channel". Court judgements seem to suggest that about two miles is the upper limit of what might be regarded as a narrow channel.

Perhaps a more useful rule of thumb is that if a channel is marked by port and starboard hand buoys, ships' watchkeepers are likely to regard it as a narrow channel.

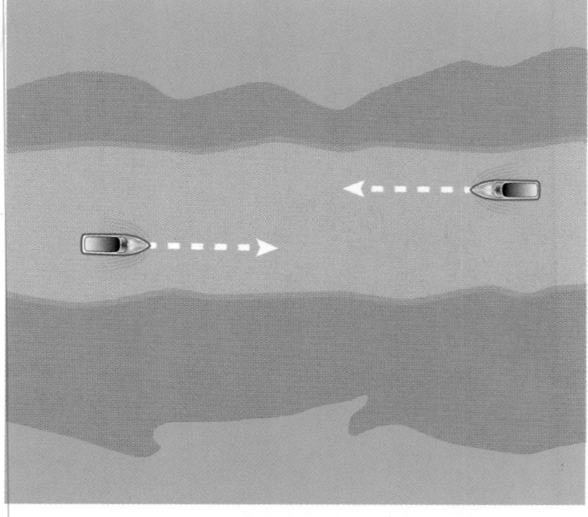

The basic rule in narrow channels is "drive on the right".

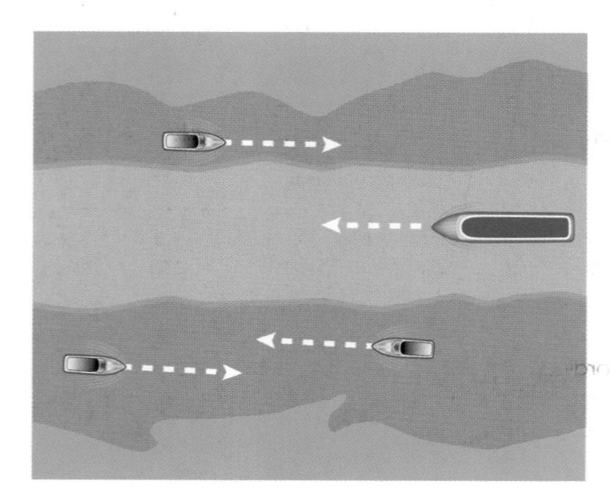

In practice

In practice, the best way to avoid impeding a large ship in a narrow channel that is marked by buoys is often to keep out of the channel altogether by staying in the shallow water, where the ships cannot go.

"Near the outer limit"

The simplistic "drive on the right" précis of this rule is open to two very different interpretations – both of which have their direct counterparts on the roads.

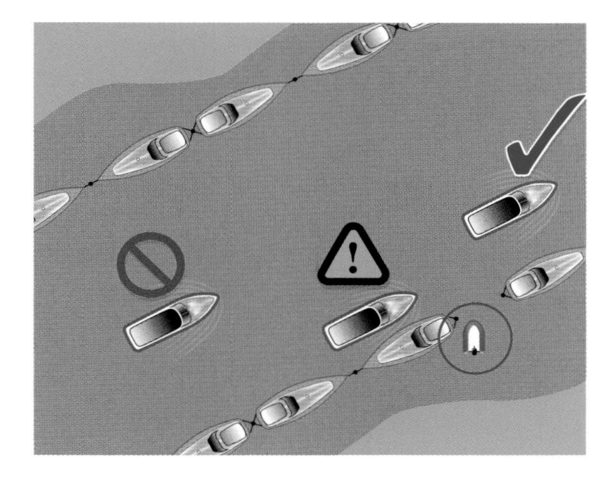

One is the "road hog" who decides to occupy the middle of the channel until oncoming traffic forces him to pull over. The other is the waterborne counterpart of the timid cyclist who rides in the gutter, wobbling over potholes and with nowhere to dodge to when a pedestrian steps off the kerb in front.

Neither is correct on the road, and neither is correct afloat.

It is summed up by the single phrase "shall keep as near to the outer limit of the channel or fairway which lies on her starboard side as is safe and practicable".

Hogging the centre or cutting corners is not "keeping near the outer limit".

But scooting along the edge of a channel with only inches to spare under your keel or with only a fender's width between your hull and a row of moored boats is not "safe and practicable". Make sure to leave yourself room to be able to alter course to starboard (i.e. further towards the edge of the channel) in case another vessel tries to dart across your path.

"Shall not impede"

"Shall not impede" is defined in the collision regulations, but not in the definitions section! It's in Rule 8.

Rule 8 f

(i) A vessel which, by any of these Rules, is required not to impede the passage or safe passage of another vessel shall, when required by the circumstances of the case, take early action to allow sufficient sea-room for the safe passage of the other vessel.

(ii) A vessel required not to impede the passage or safe passage of another vessel is not relieved of this obligation if approaching the other vessel so as to involve risk of collision and shall, when taking action, have full regard to the action which may be required by the Rules of this Part.

(iii) A vessel the passage of which is not to be impeded remains fully obliged to comply with the Rules of this Part when the two vessels are approaching one another so as to involve risk of collision.

What this means is that, as the skipper of a small craft that is required "not to impede" a larger vessel, you are expected to take avoiding action sufficiently early that the question of whether there is a risk of collision or which is the give-way vessel simply does not arise.

This is much more demanding than if we used the ordinary dictionary definition of impede, but it does not mean that you are banned from entering the channel or forced to leave it if a big ship appears. Nor does it mean that every vessel under 20m has to give way to every vessel over 20m long.

The whole thing, including the convoluted second and third paragraphs, is an expansion of an earlier and much more comprehensible guidance note that was issued by one of the IMO sub-committees and said *"a vessel that is required not to impede the passage of another shall so far as practicable navigate in such a way as to avoid the development of risk of collision. If, however, a situation has developed so as to involve risk of collision, the relevant steering and sailing rules shall be complied with"*.

Rule 10: Separation schemes

Rule 10: Traffic separation schemes

(a) This Rule applies to traffic separation schemes adopted by the Organization and does not relieve any vessel of her obligation under any other Rule.

(b) A vessel using a traffic separation scheme shall:
- (i) proceed in the appropriate traffic lane in the general direction of traffic flow for that lane;
- (ii) so far as practicable keep clear of a traffic separation line or separation zone;
- (iii) normally join or leave a traffic lane at the termination of the lane, but when joining or leaving from either side shall do so at as small an angle to the general direction of traffic flow as practicable.

(c) A vessel shall, so far as practicable, avoid crossing traffic lanes but if obliged to do so shall cross on a heading as nearly as practicable at right angles to the general direction of traffic flow.

(d)
- (i) A vessel shall not use an inshore traffic zone when she can safely use the appropriate traffic lane within the adjacent traffic separation scheme. However, vessels of less than 20 metres in length, sailing vessels and vessels engaged in fishing may use the inshore traffic zone.
- (ii) Notwithstanding sub-paragraph (d) (i), a vessel may use an inshore traffic zone when en route to or from a port, offshore installation or structure, pilot station or any other place situated within the inshore traffic zone, or to avoid immediate danger.

(e) A vessel other than a crossing vessel or a vessel joining or leaving a lane shall not normally enter a separation zone or cross a separation line except:
- (i) in cases of emergency to avoid immediate danger;
- (ii) to engage in fishing within a separation zone.

(f) A vessel navigating in areas near the terminations of traffic separation schemes shall do so with particular caution.

(g) A vessel shall so far as practicable avoid anchoring in a traffic separation scheme or in areas near its terminations.

(h) A vessel not using a traffic separation scheme shall avoid it by as wide a margin as is practicable.

(i) A vessel engaged in fishing shall not impede the passage of any vessel following a traffic lane.

(j) A vessel of less than 20 metres in length or a sailing vessel shall not impede the safe passage of a power-driven vessel following a traffic lane.

(k) A vessel restricted in her ability to manoeuvre when engaged in an operation for the maintenance of safety of navigation in a traffic separation scheme is exempted from complying with this Rule to the extent necessary to carry out the operation.

(l) A vessel restricted in her ability to manoeuvre when engaged in an operation for the laying, servicing or picking up of a submarine cable, within a traffic separation scheme, is exempted from complying with this Rule to the extent necessary to carry out the operation.

Traffic separation schemes (TSS) are clearly marked on official charts, and on most of their commercial counterparts.

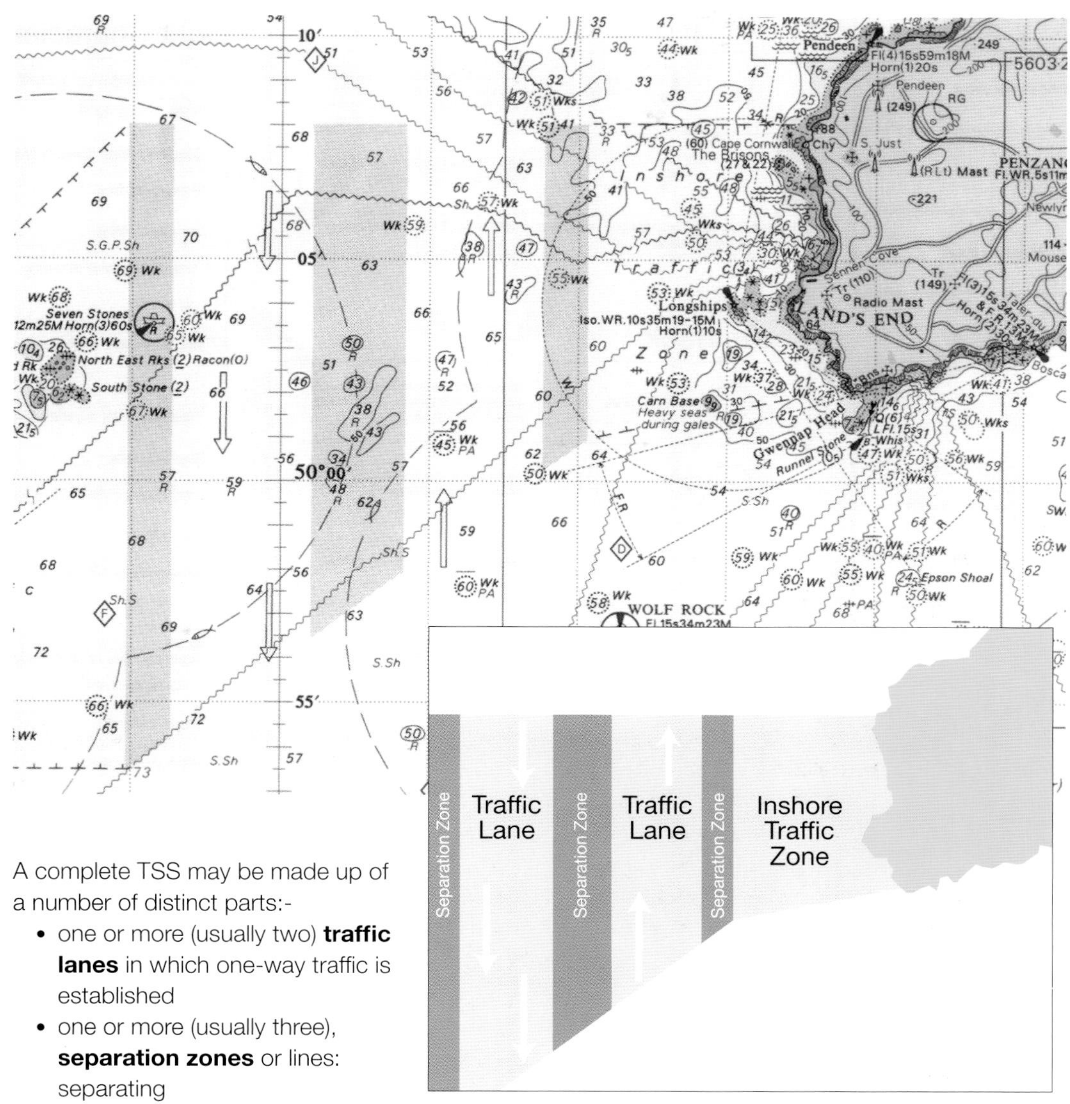

A complete TSS may be made up of a number of distinct parts:-

- one or more (usually two) **traffic lanes** in which one-way traffic is established
- one or more (usually three), **separation zones** or lines: separating
- one traffic lane from another or from the adjacent sea area if necessary, a **roundabout**: a separation point or circular separation zone and a circular traffic lane usually used at the junction between traffic separation schemes
- and usually at least one inshore traffic zone: a designated area between the landward boundary of a traffic separation scheme and the adjacent coast.

They are the maritime equivalent of dual carriageways, set up to minimise the risk of collisions in crowded shipping routes. The North Sea, in particular, is a maritime spaghetti junction of separation schemes!

Like dual carriageways, there is no obligation on anyone to use a separation scheme just because it is there: even large ships are fully entitled to go outside a separation scheme, so long as they can do so without passing through an inshore traffic zone.

The rules for vessels using a separation scheme are simple, and self-explanatory. They are required to:-

- Follow the direction of flow for the lane they are in
- Keep clear of the separation zones
- Join or leave at the ends of a scheme, or at a shallow angle (like joining a motorway!)

Although sailing vessels and power-driven vessels of less than 20 metres are not banned from separation schemes, many skippers choose to avoid them, or to take advantage of the exemption offered in paragraph 10(d)i by using the inshore traffic zone.

There are still two vital rules to be aware of:-
10j is very similar to the "shall not impede" part of Rule 9 (see page 31). The only difference is the somewhat pedantic point that it is illegal to impede **any** power-driven vessel that is following a separation lane (even one that could safely and legitimately operate outside it) whereas in a narrow channel, vessels that are capable of navigating outside the channel get no such special treatment.

For instance, a 15m sailing vessel is required not to impede a 15m motor cruiser if the motor cruiser is following a traffic lane.

Crossing at right angles

Rule 10c requires any vessel, regardless of its size or type, to cross a separation scheme "on a heading as nearly as practicable at right angles to the general direction of traffic flow".

The only exemptions are vessels involved in surveying, servicing navigation marks, or laying cables.

The key point of this rule is that it requires the **heading** to be at right angles, not the vessel's track – something that is becoming more and more significant as more small craft are fitted with track-following autopilots.

There are two very good reasons for this:-

1. It helps to make it as obvious as possible which vessels are following a traffic lane and which are crossing it.
2. It ensures that a vessel which is crossing a lane takes the shortest and supposedly the quickest route.

As is so often the case, the problem is not in the principle, but in the details: what exactly does the Rule mean by "as nearly as practicable at right angles to the general direction of traffic flow"?

One would hardly expect any official guidance about how much tolerance is given to skippers who choose to bend this rule, any more than one would expect the police to announce that they will not prosecute drivers who do 85mph on motorways. All that can be said for certain is that skippers have been prosecuted and heavily fined for crossing at sixty degrees to the traffic flow.

The MCA has made it very clear that they do not regard sailing vessels as a special case by publishing a "Guidance Note" which said

> *"No specific mention is made in the Rule of a sailing vessel having an auxiliary engine, however if such a vessel cannot follow the routeing procedures under sail because of light or adverse winds, then she should make use of her engines in order to do so and be considered as a power-driven vessel."*

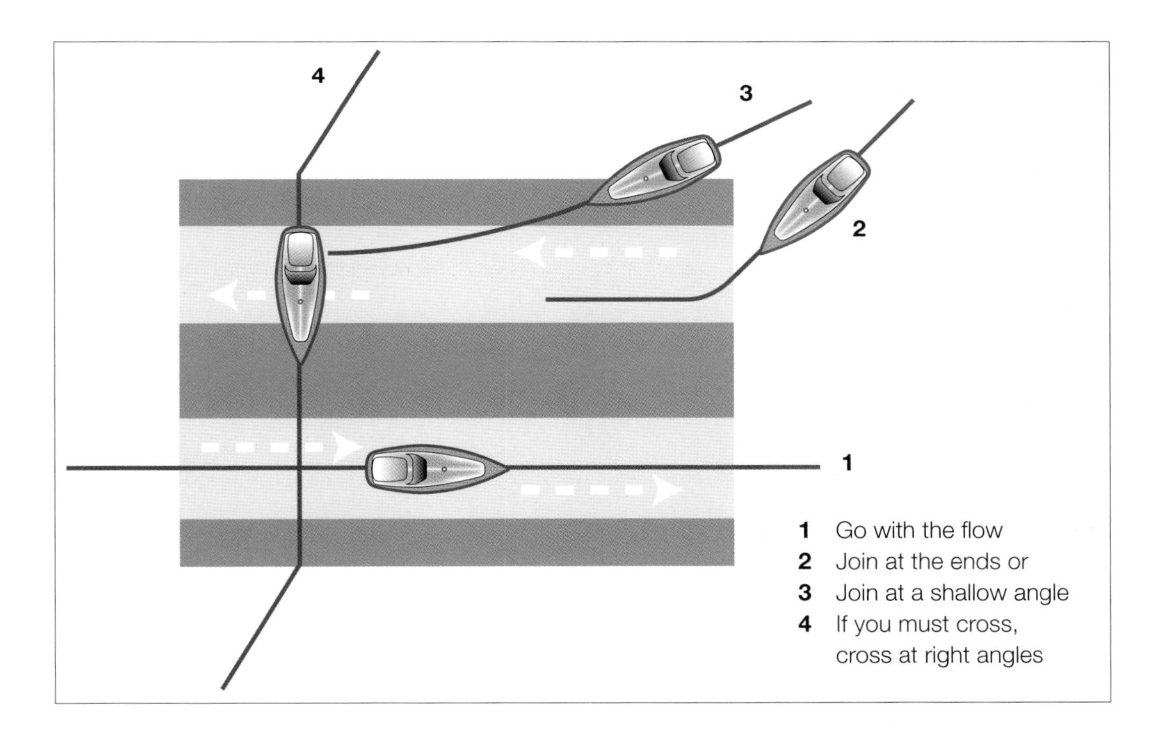

6: Fog!

Special rules in restricted visibility

The third and final section of the Steering and Sailing rules is made up of just one rule: Rule 19. It's not a particularly long or complicated rule, but when the visibility closes in, it completely replaces Rules 11-18.

That means that all the usual stuff about power giving way to sail, overtaking boats keeping clear, giving way to vessels approaching from your starboard side and such like does not apply. In particular, it is important to appreciate that there is no such thing as a "stand-on" vessel in fog.

Rule 19: Conduct of vessels in restricted visibility

(a) This Rule applies to vessels not in sight of one another when navigating in or near an area of restricted visibility.

(b) Every vessel shall proceed at a safe speed adapted to the prevailing circumstances and conditions of restricted visibility. A power-driven vessel shall have her engines ready for immediate manoeuvre.

(c) Every vessel shall have due regard to the prevailing circumstances and conditions of restricted visibility when complying with the Rules of Section I of this Part.

The first three paragraphs of the rule seem pretty self-explanatory:-

The purpose of paragraph (a) is to make it clear that this Rule applies to vessels that are not in sight of one another because of the visibility. It does not apply if the only reason you can't see the other vessel is because there is a headland or harbour wall between you! Paragraphs (b) and (c) effectively highlight the earlier rules (Rules 5, 6, and 7) concerned with keeping a lookout, maintaining a safe speed, and assessing the risk of collision.

Back in 1933, Lord Justice Scrutton came up with a very simple way of deciding upon a safe speed. He said, in effect, that you should be able to stop in half the distance that you can see. More recent court cases have highlighted the fact that Scrutton's rule is only a rough guide – it is unnecessarily severe, for instance, on very large vessels, and almost frighteningly lax on very fast, manoeuvrable ones – and it says almost nothing about sailing vessels or small power craft.

For a sailing yacht, making something in the order of five knots and able to tack or heave to within a few tens of metres, it should certainly not be taken to mean "slow down in fog". It is far more important to preserve manoeuvrability and to reduce the length of time for which you are exposed to risk. It may even mean starting the engine in order to increase speed – though the advantages of doing so need to be carefully weighed up against the fact that the engine noise may well mask any sound signals made by other vessels.

Deciding on a safe and appropriate speed in a powerboat is even more difficult, and very much depends on the characteristics of the boat itself, as well as on the conditions. Following Scrutton's "half the limit of visibility" rule could allow a sportsboat to do forty knots in 50 metres visibility – something which is clearly ridiculous. On the other hand, the strongest asset of most motor boats is their manoeuvrability: there is no point in sacrificing that – and prolonging the agony – by going too slowly.

In most "normal" fog and "typical" boats, the answer is likely to lie somewhere towards the lower end of your planing speed range.

Rule 19: Conduct of vessels in restricted visibility (cont'd)

(d) A vessel which detects by radar alone the presence of another vessel shall determine if a close-quarters situation is developing and/or risk of collision exists. If so, she shall take avoiding action in ample time, provided that when such action consists of an alteration of course, so far as possible the following shall be avoided:

(i) an alteration of course to port for a vessel forward of the beam, other than for a vessel being overtaken;

(ii) an alteration of course towards a vessel abeam or abaft the beam.

Paragraph 'd' of Rule 19 is concerned entirely with the use of radar.

So far as collision avoidance is concerned, the key feature of almost all small-craft radars is that your own vessel is always at the centre of your radar picture. If you are moving towards a stationary object, such as a buoy, the radar picture will give the impression that you are stationary and that the buoy is moving towards you. This is known as **relative motion** because the radar represents the buoy's position relative to your own vessel, rather than its fixed position on the surface of the Earth.

If you are dealing with a moving object, such as a ship, then its relative motion depends on its own movement as well as on yours.

- The movement of the **contact** across the **radar screen** is seldom an accurate representation of the **target's** movement across the **Earth**.

Using radar to assess the risk of collision

The radar's electronic bearing line (EBL) can be used as the radar equivalent of a hand bearing compass to carry out the "steady bearing" test referred to in Rule 7: if the contact representing another vessel appears to slide straight along the EBL, the implication is that it is on a steady bearing. There must, therefore, be a risk of collision, because unless someone does something to change the situation, the contact will continue to slide along the EBL until it reaches the centre of the screen – the position already occupied by your own boat.

How near is a near miss?

Even if the EBL test suggests that there is not likely to be a collision, it is useful to know how near any near miss is likely to be, using a process known as "plotting". Plotting is not an "option": Rule 7b makes it a compulsory part of the risk assessment process.

- Measure the range and bearing of the contact, using the electronic bearing line and variable range marker (EBL and VRM), and transfer them onto a paper **plotting sheet**, or use a grease pencil or dry-wipe marker to plot directly onto the glass screen of the radar itself, or onto an acetate or acrylic sheet laid over it.
- Repeat the process at regular intervals, such as every three or six minutes.
- If neither you nor the other vessel alters course or speed, the series of plots should show the contact moving at a steady speed and in a straight line. Unless one or the other of you does something to change the situation, it will continue moving at the same speed and in the same direction, so after the first few plots, it is possible to predict the contact's future movement, and from this judge how close it will get to the centre of the screen.

The distance between the centre of the screen and the line representing the predicted movement of the contact, represents the **Closest Point of Approach** – the CPA, or the nearest part of the near miss.

- If the line showing the projected movement of the contact cuts through the heading mark, the other vessel will cross ahead.
- If it does not, we are about to cross in front of the other vessel.

Using radar to avoid collision

Parts (i) and (ii) of Rule 19d give very direct instructions about how to react to a potential collision that has been detected by radar, but they are even easier to follow if they are paraphrased as positive things to do rather than as negative things to avoid.

If we rule out the option of doing nothing or changing speed, there are only two options left: either alter course to port, or alter course to starboard. So "avoid an alteration of course to port" effectively means "alter course to starboard".

On that basis, Rule 19d tells us to:-

- *alter course to starboard for a vessel forward of the beam*
- *alter course to starboard for a vessel abeam or abaft the beam on the port side*
- *alter course to port for a vessel abeam or abaft the beam on the starboard side.*

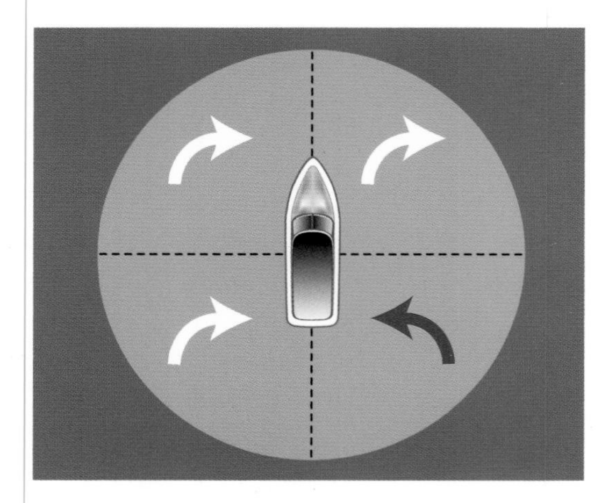

Rule 19: Conduct of vessels in restricted visibility (cont'd)

(e) Except where it has been determined that a risk of collision does not exist, every vessel which hears apparently forward of her beam the fog signal of another vessel, or which cannot avoid a close-quarters situation with another vessel forward of her beam, shall reduce her speed to the minimum at which she can be kept on her course. She shall if necessary take all her way off and in any event navigate with extreme caution until danger of collision is over.

The final part of Rule 19 applies to everyone, but it is particularly important to those without radar. It is very simple, self explanatory and common sense: if you think there is something in front of you, don't go rushing towards it!

Wahkuna
Slowing down or stopping, in fog, is not without its dangers, as the skipper and crew of a yacht called *Wahkuna* discovered in 2003, when they collided with a container ship in the English Channel.

According to the Marine Accident report *"Each vessel had detected the other by radar when at a range of about 6 miles. The container ship was on a course of 255°(T) at a speed of 25 knots. The yacht was on the port bow of the container ship on a course of 012° (C) at a speed of 7.5 knots."*

The master of the *Nedlloyd Vespucci* estimated that the yacht would pass about three quarters of a mile ahead of him. On board *Wahkuna*, things looked rather different: her skipper estimated that the container ship was likely to pass ahead of *Wahkuna*, so he reduced speed.

This apparently "concerned and confused" the master of the container ship, but he nevertheless continued at his normal service speed of 25 knots.

Minutes later, the bulbous bow of the container ship hit the almost stationary yacht demolishing the first 3m of her hull. The container ship continued on passage, while the yacht crew took to their liferaft, and were rescued, six hours later, by a passing ferry.

Rules 35 and 32: Sound signals in restricted visibility

It is tempting to think that fog signals are obsolete, now that "everyone" has radar. But of course, every one does not have radar – and even for those that do, it doesn't tell the whole story.

Fog signals still have a vital part to play in collision avoidance, particularly for small sailing vessels that are almost silent and may not be very conspicuous on radar.

Rule 35: Sound signals in restricted visibility
In or near an area of restricted visibility, whether by day or night, the signals prescribed in this Rule shall be used as follows:

(a) A power-driven vessel making way through the water shall sound at intervals of not more than 2 minutes one prolonged blast.

(b) A power-driven vessel underway but stopped and making no way through the water shall sound at intervals of not more than 2 minutes two prolonged blasts in succession with an interval of about 2 seconds between them.

(c) A vessel not under command, a vessel restricted in her ability to manoeuvre, a vessel constrained by her draught, a sailing vessel, a vessel engaged in fishing and a vessel engaged in towing or pushing another vessel shall, instead of the signals prescribed in paragraphs (a) or (b) of this Rule, sound at intervals of not more than 2 minutes three blasts in succession, namely one prolonged followed by two short blasts.

(d) A vessel engaged in fishing, when at anchor, and a vessel restricted in her ability to manoeuvre when carrying out her work at anchor, shall instead of the signals prescribed in paragraph (g) of this Rule sound the signal prescribed in paragraph (c) of this Rule.

(e) A vessel towed or if more than one vessel is towed the last vessel of the tow, if manned, shall at intervals of not more than 2 minutes sound four blasts in succession, namely one prolonged followed by three short blasts. When practicable, this signal shall be made immediately after the signal made by the towing vessel.

(f) When a pushing vessel and a vessel being pushed ahead are rigidly connected in a composite unit they shall be regarded as a power-driven vessel and shall give the signals prescribed in paragraphs (a) or (b) of this Rule.

Rule 32: Definitions

(a) The word "whistle" means any sound signalling appliance capable of producing the prescribed blasts and which complies with the specifications in Annex III to these Regulations.
(b) The term "short blast" means a blast of about one second's duration.
(c) The term "prolonged blast" means a blast of from four to six seconds' duration.

For vessels under way (including those that are "under way but not making way" – i.e. drifting) the basic rules are simple:

Under power	One five second blast on the foghorn every two minutes.	
Power driven vessel (stopped)	Two five second blasts every two minutes.	
Every one else except a vessel being towed (including sailing vessels, fishing vessels, tugs with tows, and vessels constrained by their draught)	One five second blast followed by two one second blasts (Letter D in Morse code: think of it as an abbreviation for all the lame Ducks!)	
A vessel being towed (or the last vessel in a string)	One five second blast followed by three one second blasts (Letter B in Morse code)	

Rule 35: Sound signals in restricted visibility (cont'd)

(g) A vessel at anchor shall at intervals of not more than one minute ring the bell rapidly for about 5 seconds. In a vessel of 100 metres or more in length the bell shall be sounded in the forepart of the vessel and immediately after the ringing of the bell the gong shall be sounded rapidly for about 5 seconds in the after part of the vessel. A vessel at anchor may in addition sound three blasts in succession, namely one short, one prolonged and one short blast, to give warning of her position and of the possibility of collision to an approaching vessel.
(h) A vessel aground shall give the bell signal and if required the gong signal prescribed in paragraph (g) of this Rule and shall, in addition, give three separate and distinct strokes on the bell immediately before and after the rapid ringing of the bell. A vessel aground may in addition sound an appropriate whistle signal.

At anchor (less than 100m)	Five second bell, every one minute.	
At anchor (more than 100m)	Five second bell followed by five second gong, every one minute.	
Aground (less than 100m)	Three bell strokes before and after the five-second bell, every minute.	
Optional signal for any vessel at anchor	One one-second blast, followed by one five-second blast, followed by another one-second blast (Letter R in Morse code).	

Vessels which are fishing or restricted in their ability to manoeuvre continue to sound the Morse D signal even when they are anchored, but for everyone else, the signal changes. The basic signal is five seconds rapid ringing of a bell. In ships that are more than 100 metres long, the rules specify that the bell has to be "in the forepart of the vessel", and that it has to be followed by five seconds' sounding of a gong in the after part of the vessel.

If you ever find yourself trying to pick your way through an anchorage in fog, though, it is worth bearing in mind that in a vessel less than 100 metres long, the bell may be anywhere on board.

Rule 35: Sound signals in restricted visibility (cont'd)

(i) A vessel of 12 metres or more but less than 20 metres in length shall not be obliged to give the bell signals prescribed in paragraphs (g) and (h) of this Rule. However, if she does not, she shall make some other efficient sound signal at intervals of not more than 2 minutes.

(j) A vessel of less than 12 metres in length shall not be obliged to give the above-mentioned signals but, if she does not, shall make some other efficient sound signal at intervals of not more than 2 minutes.

(k) A pilot vessel when engaged on pilotage duty may in addition to the signals prescribed in paragraphs (a),(b) or (g) of this Rule sound an identity signal consisting of four short blasts.

Until recently, all vessels over 12 metres in length were required to carry a bell. In reality, and regardless of the rules, relatively few small craft ever did so, so in 2003 the lower limit was extended to 20 metres. Instead of simply changing the 12 to 20, however, a new rule 35(i) was inserted and the previous rule moved down to 35(j).

Together, Rules 35(i) and 35(j) mean that all vessels under 20 metres long are exempt from bell-ringing in fog, but they must make "some other efficient sound signal" instead. The most obvious option, and the one least likely to be confused with anything else, is the Morse R that is given as an optional whistle signal in Rule 35(g).

7: Lights and Shapes

Rules that always apply

Together, the rules governing lights and shapes make up Part C of the collision regulations.

Lights, in the Colregs, serve three distinct purposes:-

1. they indicate the **presence** of a vessel
2. they indicate its **heading**
3. they indicate its **status** under the Colregs

"Shapes" refers to three-dimensional geometric shapes that are displayed by day, instead of lights, to indicate a vessel's status.

Rule 20: Application

Rule 20: Application

(a) Rules in this Part shall be complied with in all weathers.

(b) The Rules concerning lights shall be complied with from sunset to sunrise and during such times no other lights shall be exhibited, except such lights as cannot be mistaken for the lights specified in these Rules or do not impair their visibility or distinctive character, or interfere with the keeping of a proper look-out.

(c) The lights prescribed by these Rules shall, if carried, also be exhibited from sunrise to sunset in restricted visibility and may be exhibited in all other circumstances when it is deemed necessary.

(d) The Rules concerning shapes shall be complied with by day.

(e) The lights and shapes specified in these Rules shall comply with the provisions of Annex I to these Regulations.

Rule 20 simply tells us that lights must be displayed between sunset and sunrise and in restricted visibility, but it does not say that they have to be switched off during daylight and good visibility and specifically says that they should be switched on whenever they might be necessary.

This does not, however, mean that lights can be used as an alternative to shapes, which are compulsory by day, whether you have lights on or not.

Two other sensible but often-neglected requirements are that navigation lights should be positioned in such a way that they do not interfere with your ability to keep a proper lookout and that other lights must not obscure or be mistaken for the navigation lights.

Rule 21: Definitions

Rule 21: Definitions

(a) "Masthead light" means a white light placed over the fore and aft centreline of the vessel showing an unbroken light over an arc of the horizon of 225 degrees and so fixed as to show the light from right ahead to 22.5 degrees abaft the beam on either side of the vessel.

(b) "Sidelights" means a green light on the starboard side and a red light on the port side each showing an unbroken light over an arc of the horizon of 112.5 degrees and so fixed as to show the light from the right ahead to 22.5 degrees abaft the beam on its respective side. In a vessel of less than 20 metres in length the sidelights may be combined in one lantern carried on the fore and aft centreline of the vessel.

(c) "Sternlight" means a white light placed as nearly as practicable at the stern showing an unbroken light over an arc of the horizon of 135 degrees and so fixed as to show the light 67.5 degrees from right aft on each side of the vessel.

(d) "Towing light" means a yellow light having the same characteristics as the "sternlight" defined in paragraph (c) of this Rule.

(e) "All-round light" means a light showing an unbroken light over an arc of the horizon of 360 degrees.

(f) "Flashing light" means a light flashing at regular intervals at a frequency of 120 flashes or more per minute.

Paragraphs a, b, and c of this Rule set out the three main types of navigation light that are common to almost all vessels.

A key feature of this is that between them, they divide the water around the boat into three distinct arcs.

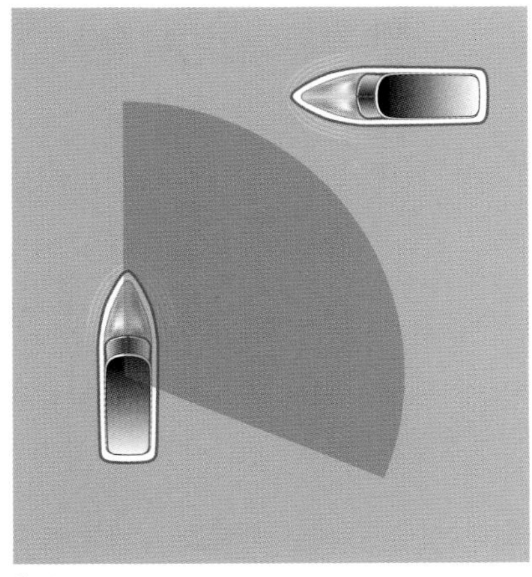

fig 1

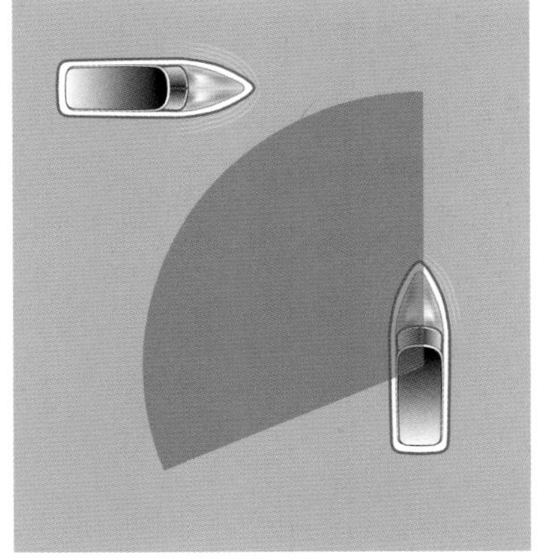

fig 2

fig 1. From directly ahead of the boat, through 112.5° to just abaft the starboard beam is covered by a green light. If you compare this with the obligations of a power-driven vessel meeting another power-driven vessel in Rule 14 (page 22) you will see that you are required to give way to anyone approaching in this sector. In other words, a **stand-on vessel will see a green sidelight**.

fig 2. From directly ahead of the boat, through 112.5° to just abaft the port beam is covered by a red light. Now, if you compare this with the obligations when two power-driven vessels are crossing, (Rule 14 on page 22) you will see that anyone approaching in this sector is required to give way to you. In other words, **a give-way vessel will see a red sidelight**.

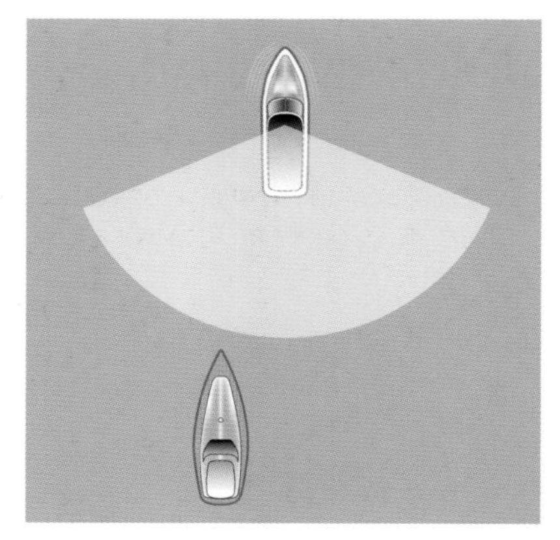

The arc not covered by the sidelights is filled in by the stern light. It is sometimes known as an "overtaking light" because it exactly matches the overtaking sector set out in Rule 13 (see page 16). In other words, an overtaking vessel will see a white sternlight.

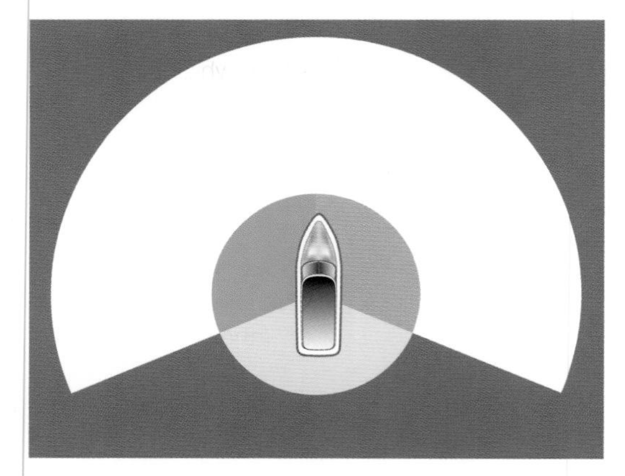

Masthead lights are still sometimes called "steaming lights", because they are shown only by power-driven vessels.

They cover exactly the same arc as the two sidelights put together, but are much brighter, and can be seen over considerably greater distances.

Rule 22: Visibility of lights

Rule 22: Visibility of lights

The lights prescribed in these Rules shall have an intensity as specified in Section 8 of Annex I to these Regulations so as to be visible at the following minimum ranges:

(a) In vessels of 50 metres or more in length:
a masthead light, 6 miles;
a sidelight, 3 miles;
a sternlight, 3 miles;
a towing light, 3 miles;
a white, red, green or yellow all-round light, 3 miles.

(b) In vessels of 12 metres or more in length but less than 50 metres in length:
a masthead light, 5 miles; except that where the length of the vessel is less than 20 metres, 3 miles;
a sidelight, 2 miles;
a sternlight, 2 miles;
a towing light, 2 miles;
a white, red, green or yellow all-round light, 2 miles.

(c) In vessels of less than 12 metres in length:
a masthead light, 2 miles;
a sidelight, 1 mile;
a sternlight, 2 miles;
a towing light, 2 miles;
a white, red, green or yellow all-round light, 2 miles.

(d) In inconspicuous, partly submerged vessels or objects being towed:
a white all-round light, 3 miles.

Rule 22 sets out the range over which each type of navigation light should be visible in good visibility: a formula for converting these nominal ranges into luminous intensity is given in Annex 1.

As one might expect, the intensity of lights required is linked to the size of the vessel: a small boat that is dependent on a 12-volt battery cannot be expected to display lights as bright as those of a large ship.

But it is important for the skippers of small craft – particularly small sailing vessels – to appreciate that by the time their sidelights are visible to the watchkeeper of an approaching ship, time and sea-room may already be running out. If the battery voltage is low, if the wiring or connections are corroded, or if the lights' lenses are cracked, crazed, or dirty, or even if the boat is heeling over by more than a few degrees, you may be effectively invisible until it is too late.

Ouzo

In August 2006, the bodies of three yachtsmen were recovered from the sea, just off the Isle of Wight. They were quickly traced back to the 25 foot sailing yacht *Ouzo* – but of *Ouzo* herself, there was no sign. Even so, accident investigators eventually decided that the ferry *Pride of Bilbao* had either collided with *Ouzo* or had passed so close to her that the yacht had been swamped or capsized by the vessel's wash. They concluded that *"any attempts the yachtsmen might have made to attract the ferry's attention were ineffective as the ferry's watchkeeping officer and lookout only saw the yacht's lights at the last minute, by which time they were unable to keep well clear. The yacht had not shown up on the ferry's radars despite probably having a radar reflector hoisted."*

A leaflet published by the Marine Accident Investigation Branch in the wake of its report suggested:-

1. Yachts cannot be seen easily from the bridges of ships, and yachtsmen need to be proactive in attracting the attention of the ships' watchkeepers. **Yachtsmen should not hesitate to attract the attention of ships' watchkeepers by whatever means are available**.

2. The lookout on the ferry had not seen the yacht until it was very close ahead.
   - The lenses of navigation lights are prone to crazing which substantially reduces their efficiency.
   - The bulbs fitted to navigation lights can easily be inadvertently replaced with bulbs of a lower rating.
   - It is quite common for replacement bulbs to have damaged filaments, which cause an intermittent fault.
   - If the yacht heels more than 5° the horizontal intensity of her navigation lights may be decreased.

Yacht owners should make every effort to ensure that their navigation lights are fully effective, and their characteristics understood.

Rules 23 to 31: Who shows what?

Rules 23 to 31, and their predecessors, have blighted the lives of generations of Cadets and Midshipmen! Accounting for almost a third of the Colregs word-count, they list every light and shape for every kind of vessel from a rowing dinghy to a supertanker – including seaplanes and submerged objects under tow!

In fact, the Rules are less complicated than they seem: in general, and with very few significant exceptions

- any vessel that is moving shows sidelights and a stern light
- any vessel that is proceeding under its own power shows masthead lights
- any vessel that is claiming special status shows additional all-round lights.

The most common problem is usually picking out the navigation lights from a mass of deck and accommodation lights.

Rule 23: Power-driven vessels underway

(a) A power-driven vessel underway shall exhibit:
  (i) a masthead light forward;
  (ii) a second masthead light abaft of and higher than the forward one; except that a vessel of less than 50 metres in length shall not be obliged to exhibit such light but may do so;
  (iii) sidelights;
  (iv) a sternlight.

(b) An air-cushion vessel when operating in the non-displacement mode shall, in addition to the lights prescribed in paragraph (a) of this Rule, exhibit an all-round flashing yellow light.

(c) A WIG craft only when taking off, landing and in flight near the surface shall, in addition to the lights prescribed in paragraph (a) of this Rule, exhibit a high intensity all-round flashing red light.

(d)
  (i) A power-driven vessel of less than 12 metres in length may in lieu of the lights prescribed in paragraph (a) of this Rule exhibit an all-round white light and sidelights;
  (ii) a power-driven vessel of less than 7 metres in length whose maximum speed does not exceed 7 knots may in lieu of the lights prescribed in paragraph (a) of this Rule exhibit an all-round white light and shall, if practicable, also exhibit sidelights;
  (iii) the masthead light or all-round white light on a power-driven vessel of less than 12 metres in length may be displaced from the fore and aft centreline of the vessel if centreline fitting is not practicable, provided that the sidelights are combined in one lantern which shall be carried on the fore and aft centreline of the vessel or located as nearly as practicable in the same fore and aft line as the masthead light or the all-round white light.

Power-driven vessel under 50m: Port bow

Power-driven vessel under 50m: Astern

A power-driven vessel of less than 50 metres in length carries the four basic lights: a green starboard sidelight; a red port sidelight, a white sternlight, and a white masthead light.

Power-driven vessel over 50m: Port bow

Power-driven vessel over 50m: Astern

A power-driven vessel over 50 metres in length carries the four basic lights, plus a second masthead light. The forward masthead light is always the lower of the two.

Small power-driven vessel: Port bow

Small power-driven vessel: Astern

Power-driven vessels less than 20m in length are allowed to carry a single "combined lantern", fitted with a two-colour lens to show a red light to port and a green light to starboard, instead of separate sidelights. Power-driven vessels less than 12m in length are allowed to display an all-round white light instead of separate masthead and stern lights.

WIG craft: Port bow

WIG craft: Starboard quarter

WIG craft are "Wing in Ground-effect aircraft" – very low-flying seaplanes.

When operating on the surface, a WIG craft must show the lights of a conventional power-driven vessel of the same size, but when it is taking off, or landing or in low-level flight, it must add an all-round flashing red light.

Air cushion vessel: Port aspect

Air cushion vessel: Astern

An air cushion vessel (hovercraft) shows the lights of a conventional power driven vessel of the same size, but with the addition of an all-round flashing yellow light.

Rule 24: Towing and pushing

(a) A power-driven vessel when towing shall exhibit:

(i) instead of the light prescribed in Rule 23(a)(i) or (a)(ii), two masthead lights in a vertical line. When the length of the tow, measuring from the stern of the towing vessel to the after end of the tow exceeds 200 metres, three such lights in a vertical line;

(ii) sidelights;

(iii) a sternlight;

(iv) a towing light in a vertical line above the sternlight;

(v) when the length of the tow exceeds 200 metres, a diamond shape where it can best be seen.

(b) When a pushing vessel and a vessel being pushed ahead are rigidly connected in a composite unit they shall be regarded as a power-driven vessel and exhibit the lights prescribed in Rule 23.

(c) A power-driven vessel when pushing ahead or towing alongside, except in the case of a composite unit, shall exhibit:

(i) instead of the light prescribed in Rule 23(a)(i) or (a)(ii), two masthead lights in a vertical line;

(ii) sidelights;

(iii) a sternlight.

(d) A power-driven vessel to which paragraph (a) or (c) of this Rule applies shall also comply with Rule 23(a)(ii).

(e) A vessel or object being towed, other than those mentioned in paragraph (g) of this Rule, shall exhibit:

(i) sidelights;

(ii) a sternlight;

(iii) when the length of the tow exceeds 200 metres, a diamond shape where it can best be seen.

(f) Provided that any number of vessels being towed alongside or pushed in a group shall be lighted as one vessel,

(i) a vessel being pushed ahead, not being part of a composite unit, shall exhibit at the forward end sidelights;

(ii) a vessel being towed alongside shall exhibit a sternlight and at the forward end, sidelights.

(g) An inconspicuous, partly submerged vessel or object, or combination of such vessels or objects being towed, shall exhibit:

(i) if it is less than 25 metres in breadth, one all-round white light at or near the forward end and one at or near the after end except that dracones need not exhibit a light at or near the forward end;

(ii) if it is 25 metres or more in breadth, two additional all-round white lights at or near the extremities of its breadth;

(iii) if it exceeds 100 metres in length, additional all-round white lights between the lights prescribed in sub-paragraphs (i) and (ii) so that the distance between the lights shall not exceed 100 metres;

(iv) a diamond shape at or near the aftermost extremity of the last vessel or object being towed and if the length of the tow exceeds 200 metres an additional diamond shape where it can best be seen and located as far forward as is practicable.

(h) Where from any sufficient cause it is impracticable for a vessel or object being towed to exhibit the lights or shapes prescribed in paragraph (e) or (g) of this Rule, all possible measures shall be taken to light the vessel or object towed or at least to indicate the presence of such vessel or object.

(i) Where from any sufficient cause it is impracticable for a vessel not normally engaged in towing operations to display the lights prescribed in paragraph (a) or (c) of this Rule, such vessel shall not be required to exhibit those lights when engaged in towing another vessel in distress or otherwise in need of assistance. All possible measures shall be taken to indicate the nature of the relationship between the towing vessel and the vessel being towed as authorized by Rule 36, in particular by illuminating the towline.

Tug and short tow: Port bow

Tug and short tow: Starboard quarter

The tug is a power-driven vessel, so it shows the four basic lights. Its special status is indicated by an extra steaming light, vertically below the first. A steaming light, however, is not visible to vessels approaching from astern, so the vital stern sector is "filled in" by a yellow towing light immediately above the sternlight.

The tow, meanwhile, is moving, so it shows the usual side and stern lights, but it is not under its own power, so it does not show a steaming light. Some people find it helpful to imagine that the tow has "given its steaming light to the tug".

If the tug is pushing, or towing alongside, the tug and tow show the same lights, except that the tug does not show its yellow towing light.

Tug and long tow: Port bow

Tug and long tow: Starboard quarter

If the length of the tow, measured from the stern of the tug to the stern of the tow, is more than 200 metres, the tug has to display a third steaming light, in the same vertical line as the other two. Otherwise, by night, the rules are the same as for a shorter tow: the tug displays a towing light in addition to its normal lights, and each vessel in the tow displays side and stern lights but no steaming light.

By day, however, the tug and the last vessel of a long tow must both display a black diamond day-shape.

Tug and submerged tow: Port bow

It is impractical to expect partially submerged objects to carry and display a full set of navigation lights, so they are required, instead, to be marked with all-round white lights displayed at the front and back of the tow, and at intervals of not more than 100 metres in between.

Rule 25 : Sailing vessels underway and vessels under oars

(a) A sailing vessel underway shall exhibit:
  (i) sidelights;
  (ii) a sternlight.

(b) In a sailing vessel of less than 20 metres in length the lights prescribed in paragraph (a) of this Rule may be combined in one lantern carried at or near the top of the mast where it can best be seen.

(c) A sailing vessel underway may, in addition to the lights prescribed in paragraph (a) of this Rule, exhibit at or near the top of the mast, where they can best be seen, two all-round lights in a vertical line, the upper being red and the lower green, but these lights shall not be exhibited in conjunction with the combined lantern permitted by paragraph (b) of this Rule.

(d)
  (i) A sailing vessel of less than 7 metres in length shall, if practicable, exhibit the lights prescribed in paragraph (a) or (b) of this Rule, but if she does not, she shall have ready at hand an electric torch or lighted lantern showing a white light which shall be exhibited in sufficient time to prevent collision.
  (ii) A vessel under oars may exhibit the lights prescribed in this Rule for sailing vessels, but if she does not, she shall have ready at hand an electric torch or lighted lantern showing a white light which shall be exhibited in sufficient time to prevent collision.

(e) A vessel proceeding under sail when also being propelled by machinery shall exhibit forward where it can best be seen a conical shape, apex downwards.

Sailing vessels: Port aspect

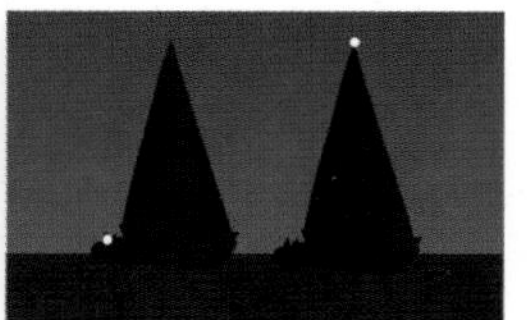

Sailing vessels: Starboard quarter

A sailing vessel must conform to the general principles by showing sidelights and a sternlight, but as it is propelled by the wind, rather than by its own machinery, it does not show a masthead "steaming" light.

Like their power-driven counterparts, sailing vessels of less than 20m in length are allowed to carry a single "combined lantern", fitted with a two-colour lens to show a red light to port and a green light to starboard, instead of separate sidelights. Or they can go a stage further, with a tricolour lantern at the masthead that combines the functions of both sidelights and the sternlight.

The height and power-saving achieved by a masthead tricolour makes it a very popular and useful option, particularly in open water, but it is not without its drawbacks.

The first of these is that the failure of its single, rather inaccessible bulb can render you invisible unless you have a back-up system.

A deck-level back-up system is also useful in many small harbours, where you may be operating so close to other small craft that a masthead-mounted tricolour may be too high to be noticed.

And finally, if you have an engine, deck-level sidelights and sternlight are essential because the masthead tricolour cannot be used with a masthead "steaming" light when operating under power.

Sailing vessels: Port aspect

Sailing vessels: Starboard quarter

A sailing vessel does not have to show any extra lights, but has the option of displaying all-round red and green lights at the masthead. In practice, the optional sailing lights are almost entirely confined to large sailing vessels, but there is no lower limit to their use, so long as they are not used in conjunction with a tricolour combined lantern.

Vessels under 7 metres

Sailing vessels under 7 metres in length, vessels under oars, and power vessels of less than 7 metres whose maximum design speed is less than 7 knots are all exempt from the general requirement to display sidelights and stern lights. Small power-driven vessels (such as outboard-powered tenders) must show an all-round white light. For small sailing boats and vessels of any size under oars, the rules are relaxed even further: they are required only to have "ready at hand an electric torch or lighted lantern showing a white light which shall be exhibited in sufficient time to prevent collision".

Motor-sailing

A vessel proceeding under sail when also being propelled by machinery – motor-sailing – is not classed as a sailing vessel. From the moment her engine is put in gear, she becomes a power-driven vessel, and at night, should show the appropriate lights. On the vast majority of yachts, this involves switching the masthead tricolour off, and replacing it with low-level sidelights and sternlight, as well as switching the masthead "steaming" light on.

By day, a vessel that is motor-sailing should show a black cone, apex downwards, "forward where it can best be seen". Unlike the rules regarding lights, there are few concessions for small craft regarding shapes. On vessels of less than 20 metres in length, shapes can be less than the standard 0.6m diameter (see Annex 1.6) but they must still be "commensurate with the size of the vessel".

Strictly speaking, even a sailing dinghy with an outboard motor should have a small black cone ready to display when the outboard is in use!

Rule 26: Fishing Vessels

(a) A vessel engaged in fishing, whether underway or at anchor, shall exhibit only the lights and shapes prescribed in this Rule.

(b) A vessel when engaged in trawling, by which is meant the dragging through the water of a dredge net or other apparatus used as a fishing appliance, shall exhibit:

(i) two all-round lights in a vertical line, the upper being green and the lower white, or a shape consisting of two cones with their apexes together in a vertical line one above the other;

(ii) a masthead light abaft of and higher than the all-round green light; a vessel of less than 50 metres in length shall not be obliged to exhibit such a light but may do so;

(iii) when making way through the water, in addition to the lights prescribed in this paragraph, sidelights and a sternlight.

(c) A vessel engaged in fishing, other than trawling, shall exhibit:

(i) two all-round lights in a vertical line, the upper being red and the lower white, or a shape consisting of two cones with apexes together in a vertical line one above the other;

(ii) when there is outlying gear extending more than 150 metres horizontally from the vessel, an all-round white light or a cone apex upwards in the direction of the gear;

(iii) when making way through the water, in addition to the lights prescribed in this paragraph, sidelights and a sternlight.

(d) The additional signals described in Annex II to these Regulations apply to a vessel engaged in fishing in close proximity to other vessels engaged in fishing.

(e) A vessel when not engaged in fishing shall not exhibit the lights or shapes prescribed in this Rule, but only those prescribed for a vessel of her length.

So far as the Colregs are concerned, there are only two kinds of fishing vessels:-

- trawlers, which drag nets or dredges behind them
- and others – which don't, and whose gear may extend sideways or forwards.

Sea angling boats and others whose gear does not restrict their manoeuvrability are not classed as fishing vessels.

Other signals may be used by fishing vessels operating in close proximity to each other: they are of little significance to other vessels, but details are included in Annex 2 to the collision regulations, on page 67.

By day, all fishing vessels whose gear restricts their ability to manoeuvre are supposed to display two black cones, point to point.

In theory – though seldom in practice – the cones should be removed when the vessel is not actively engaged in fishing.

Trawler: Port aspect

Trawler: Astern

Other fishing vessel: Port aspect

Other fishing vessel: Astern

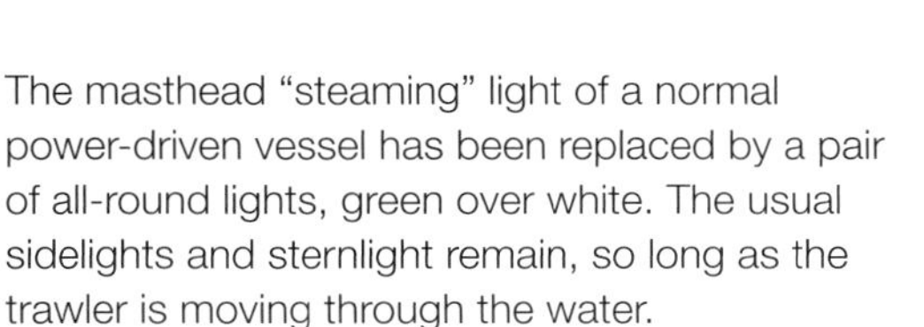

The masthead "steaming" light of a normal power-driven vessel has been replaced by a pair of all-round lights, green over white. The usual sidelights and sternlight remain, so long as the trawler is moving through the water.

Like a trawler, the masthead "steaming" light of a normal power-driven vessel has been replaced by a pair of all-round lights, but here the upper light is red instead of green. Again, the usual side-lights and sternlight remain, so long as the vessel is moving through the water.

Rule 27: Vessels not under command or restricted in their ability to manoeuvre

(a) A vessel not under command shall exhibit:
- (i) two all-round red lights in a vertical line where they can best be seen;
- (ii) two balls or similar shapes in a vertical line where they can best be seen;
- (iii) when making way through the water, in addition to the lights prescribed in this paragraph, sidelights and a sternlight.

(b) A vessel restricted in her ability to manoeuvre, except a vessel engaged in mine-clearance operations, shall exhibit:
- (i) three all-round lights in a vertical line where they can best be seen. The highest and lowest of these lights shall be red and the middle light shall be white;
- (ii) three shapes in a vertical line where they can best be seen. The highest and lowest of these shapes shall be balls and the middle one a diamond;
- (iii) when making way through the water, a masthead light or lights, sidelights and a sternlight, in addition to the lights prescribed in sub-paragraph (i);
- (iv) when at anchor, in addition to the lights or shapes prescribed in sub-paragraphs (i) and (ii), the light, lights or shape prescribed in Rule 30.

(c) A power-driven vessel engaged in a towing operation such as severely restricts the towing vessel and her tow in their ability to deviate from their course shall, in addition to the lights or shapes prescribed in Rule 24(a), exhibit the lights or shapes prescribed in sub-paragraphs (b)(i) and (ii) of this Rule.

Vessel not under command: starboard bow

A vessel that is unable to manoeuvre because of some unforeseen circumstance such as a mechanical failure shows two red lights in a vertical line. If it is moving, it adds sidelights and a sternlight, but not masthead lights.

Vessel restricted in its ability to manoeuvre: starboard bow

All sorts of vessels may be involved in jobs that restrict their ability to manoeuvre: they include pipe and cable layers, dredgers, survey vessels, buoy-layers, ships refuelling at sea, launching aircraft, or engaged in a particularly difficult tow.

All of them display three all-round lights, red, white, and red in a vertical line, in addition to their normal navigation lights.

The corresponding day shape consists of a ball, diamond and ball, in a vertical line. Be aware, however, that a shape 0.6m in diameter – the standard minimum size for any vessel over 20m long – is hardly conspicuous, particularly when seen against a background of masts, funnels, and aerials.

These two ships, for instance, are both correctly displaying the day signal – but the fact that they are so close together and have a hose between them is probably more noticeable!

Rule 27: Vessels not under command or restricted in their ability to manoeuvre (cont'd)

(d) A vessel engaged in dredging or underwater operations, when restricted in her ability to manoeuvre, shall exhibit the lights and shapes prescribed in sub-paragraphs (b) (i), (ii) and (iii) of this Rule and shall in addition, when an obstruction exists, exhibit:

- (i) two all-round red lights or two balls in a vertical line to indicate the side on which the obstruction exists;
- (ii) two all-round green lights or two diamonds in a vertical line to indicate the side on which another vessel may pass;
- (iii) when at anchor, the lights or shapes prescribed in this paragraph instead of the lights or shape prescribed in Rule 30.

Vessel restricted in its ability to manoeuvre (dredging): starboard bow

A dredger shows the distinctive all-round red-white-red lights of a vessel restricted in its ability to manoeuvre, and if it is dredging while under way, it will also show its normal sidelights, sternlight, and masthead light. If it is anchored, however, it will not show anchor lights.

Additional lights, arranged in vertical pairs, may be used to indicate the presence of an obstruction: red lights on the obstructed side, and green on the clear side. By day, the ball-diamond-ball shapes replace the red-white-red lights, and black balls replace the red obstruction lights.

Rule 27: Vessels not under command or restricted in their ability to manoeuvre (cont'd)

(e) Whenever the size of a vessel engaged in diving operations makes it impracticable to exhibit all lights and shapes prescribed in paragraph (d) of this Rule, the following shall be exhibited:

(i) three all-round lights in a vertical line where they can best be seen. The highest and lowest of these lights shall be red and the middle light shall be white;

(ii) a rigid replica of the International Code flag "A" not less than 1 metre in height. Measures shall be taken to ensure its all-round visibility.

The rules governing the signals to be displayed by small craft involved in diving operations are very simple, but are frequently ignored by the very people whose lives may depend on them.

By day, the rules call for "a rigid replica of the International Code flag "A" not less than 1 metre in height".

- under-sized flags don't qualify
- fabric flags don't qualify
- other flags don't qualify

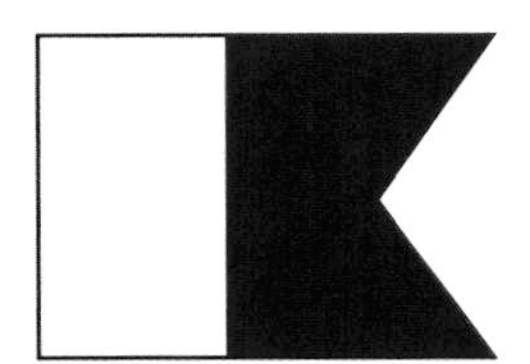

A red flag with a white diagonal stripe was invented and marketed by a private individual in the 1950s, and although it has since been made a legal requirement for diving tenders in some American states, it has no official status elsewhere or in international law. Nevertheless, many divers regard it as "the dive flag".

Rule 27: Vessels not under command or restricted in their ability to manoeuvre (cont'd)

(f) A vessel engaged in mine-clearance operations shall in addition to the lights prescribed for a power-driven vessel in Rule 23 or to the lights or shape prescribed for a vessel at anchor in Rule 30 as appropriate, exhibit three all-round green lights or three balls. One of these lights or shapes shall be exhibited near the foremast head and one at each end of the fore yard. These lights or shapes indicate that it is dangerous for another vessel to approach within 1000 metres of the mine clearance vessel.

(g) Vessels of less than 12 metres in length, except those engaged in diving operations, shall not be required to exhibit the lights and shapes prescribed in this Rule.

(h) The signals prescribed in this Rule are not signals of vessels in distress and requiring assistance. Such signals are contained in Annex IV to these Regulations.

Vessel restricted in its ability to manoeuvre (mine clearance): starboard bow

Rule 28: Vessels constrained by their draught

A vessel constrained by her draught may, in addition to the lights prescribed for power-driven vessels in Rule 23, exhibit where they can best be seen three all-round red lights in a vertical line, or a cylinder.

Vessel constrained by its draught: starboard bow

Although the rules give extra responsibilities and privileges to vessels constrained by their draught, the lights and shapes – three vertical red lights or a black cylinder – are optional.

The spacing of the lights in the illustration has been grossly exaggerated for the sake of clarity, though in practice they are still usually quite distinctive. The photograph, however, shows how difficult it can be to spot a black cylinder just 0.6m in diameter on such a large vessel.

Rule 29: Pilot vessels

(a) A vessel engaged on pilotage duty shall exhibit:
   (i) at or near the masthead, two all-round lights in a vertical line, the upper being white and the lower red;
   (ii) when underway, in addition, sidelights and a sternlight;
   (iii) when at anchor, in addition to the lights prescribed in sub-paragraph (i), the light, lights or shape prescribed in Rule 30 for vessels at anchor.

(b) A pilot vessel when not engaged on pilotage duty shall exhibit the lights or shapes prescribed for a similar vessel of her length.

Pilot vessels have no special rights or responsibilities under the collision regulations, but are to be treated as ordinary power-driven vessels. They do, however, carry special identifying lights. Unfortunately, the lights of a pilot vessel are easily confused with those of a fishing vessel, because they are the same colours – red and white – but the other way up.

Various mnemonics have been devised to help remember which is which, but poems such as "red over white means frying tonight" are probably less helpful than the fact that pilot boats operate at much higher speeds than fishing boats.

Rule 30: Anchored vessels and vessels aground

(a) A vessel at anchor shall exhibit where it can best be seen:
  (i) in the fore part, an all-round white light or one ball;
  (ii) at or near the stern and at a lower level than the light prescribed in sub-paragraph (i), an all-round white light.

(b) A vessel of less than 50 metres in length may exhibit an all-round white light where it can best be seen instead of the lights prescribed in paragraph (a) of this Rule.

(c) A vessel at anchor may, and a vessel of 100 metres and more in length shall, also use the available working or equivalent lights to illuminate her decks.

Anchored vessel: starboard bow

At night, an anchored vessel must show either one or two all-round white anchor lights: one if it is less than 50m long, and two if it is more than 50m long. If two lights are shown, then the forward one must be higher than the aft one: this is the other way round, compared with the masthead lights that would be shown when under way.

Ships over 100 metres in length are also required to leave their deck lights on.

By day, all vessels over 7 metres long are required to display a black ball in the forward part of the vessel.

Rule 30: Anchored vessels and vessels aground (cont'd)

(d) A vessel aground shall exhibit the lights prescribed in paragraph (a) or (b) of this Rule and in addition, where they can best be seen:
  (i) two all-round red lights in a vertical line;
  (ii) three balls in a vertical line.

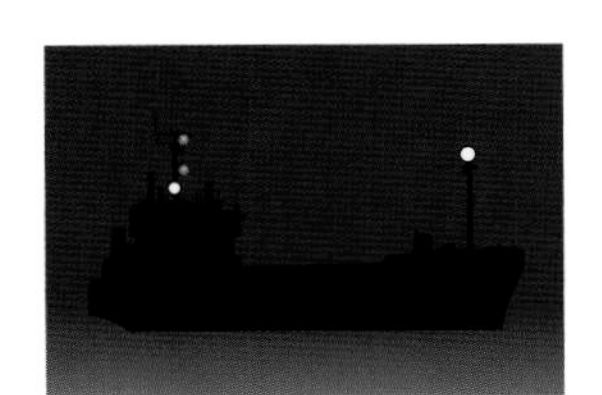

Vessel aground: starboard bow

Although vessels are not always run aground by accident or breakdown, the easiest way to remember the lights or shapes of a vessel aground is to think of them as a combination of "anchored" and "not under command" together.

Rule 30: Anchored vessels and vessels aground (cont'd)

(e) A vessel of less than 7 metres in length, when at anchor, not in or near a narrow channel, fairway or anchorage, or where other vessels normally navigate, shall not be required to exhibit the lights or shape prescribed in paragraphs (a) and (b) of this Rule.

(f) A vessel of less than 12 metres in length, when aground, shall not be required to exhibit the lights or shapes prescribed in sub-paragraphs (d) (i) and (ii) of this Rule.

Rule 31: Seaplanes

Where it is impracticable for a seaplane or a WIG craft to exhibit lights and shapes of the characteristics or in the positions prescribed in the Rules of this Part she shall exhibit lights and shapes as closely similar in characteristics and position as is possible.

8: Manoeuvring Signals
Rules that always apply

Part D of the regulations contains just six rules, one of which is concerned exclusively with fog signals (see page 41) and one of which refers to Annex IV, dealing with distress signals.

PART D - SOUND AND LIGHT SIGNALS

Rule 32: Definitions

(a) The word "whistle" means any sound signalling appliance capable of producing the prescribed blasts and which complies with the specifications in Annex III to these Regulations.
(b) The term "short blast" means a blast of about one second's duration.
(c) The term "prolonged blast" means a blast of from four to six seconds' duration.

These definitions apply to fog signals (see page 41) as well as to manoeuvring signals.

Rule 33: Equipment for sound signals

(a) A vessel of 12 metres or more in length shall be provided with a whistle, a vessel of 20 metres or more in length shall be provided with a bell in addition to a whistle, and a vessel of 100 metres or more in length shall, in addition, be provided with a gong, the tone and sound of which cannot be confused with that of the bell. The whistle, bell and gong shall comply with the specifications in Annex III to these Regulations. The bell or gong or both may be replaced by other equipment having the same respective sound characteristics, provided that manual sounding of the prescribed signals shall always be possible.
(b) A vessel of less than 12 metres in length shall not be obliged to carry the sound signalling appliances prescribed in paragraph (a) of this Rule but if she does not, she shall be provided with some other means of making an efficient sound signal.

Rule 34: Manoeuvring and warning signals

(a) When vessels are in sight of one another, a power-driven vessel underway, when manoeuvring as authorized or required by these Rules, shall indicate that manoeuvre by the following signals on her whistle:
one short blast to mean "I am altering my course to starboard";
two short blasts to mean "I am altering my course to port";
three short blasts to mean "I am operating astern propulsion".
(b) Any vessel may supplement the whistle signals prescribed in paragraph (a) of this Rule by light signals, repeated as appropriate, whilst the manoeuvre is being carried out:
(i) these light signals shall have the following significance:
one flash to mean "I am altering my course to starboard";
two flashes to mean "I am altering my course to port";
three flashes to mean "I am operating astern propulsion";
(ii) the duration of each flash shall be about one second, the interval between flashes shall be about one second, and the interval between successive signals shall be not less than ten seconds;
(iii) the light used for this signal shall, if fitted, be an all-round white light, visible at a minimum range of 5 miles, and shall comply with the provisions of Annex I to these Regulations.

I am altering course to starboard	One one-second blast may be accompanied by one one-second flash of an all-round white light.	
I am altering course to port	Two one-second blasts may be accompanied by two one-second flashes.	
I am operating astern propulsion – but not necessarily "I am going backwards"	Three one-second blasts may be accompanied by three one-second flashes.	

Rule 34: Manoeuvring and warning signals (cont'd)

(c) When in sight of one another in a narrow channel or fairway:

(i) a vessel intending to overtake another shall in compliance with Rule 9(e)(i) indicate her intention by the following signals on her whistle:
two prolonged blasts followed by one short blast to mean "I intend to overtake you on your starboard side";
two prolonged blasts followed by two short blasts to mean "I intend to overtake you on your port side".

(ii) the vessel about to be overtaken when acting in accordance with Rule 9(e)(i) shall indicate her agreement by the following signal on her whistle:
one prolonged, one short, one prolonged and one short blast, in that order.

"I intend to overtake you on your starboard side"		
"I intend to overtake you on your port side"		
Reply: "Yes, you may overtake"	Morse code "C" – means "yes" may be accompanied by corresponding flashes of an all-round white light.	

Rule 34: Manoeuvring and warning signals (cont'd)

(d) When vessels in sight of one another are approaching each other and from any cause either vessel fails to understand the intentions or actions of the other, or is in doubt whether sufficient action is being taken by the other to avoid collision, the vessel in doubt shall immediately indicate such doubt by giving at least five short and rapid blasts on the whistle. Such signal may be supplemented by a light signal of at least five short and rapid flashes.

"I do not understand your intentions"		

Rule 34: Manoeuvring and warning signals (cont'd)

(e) A vessel nearing a bend or an area of a channel or fairway where other vessels may be obscured by an intervening obstruction shall sound one prolonged blast. Such signal shall be answered with a prolonged blast by any approaching vessel that may be within hearing around the bend or behind the intervening obstruction.

Approaching a blind bend or obstruction		

Rule 34: Manoeuvring and warning signals (cont'd)

(f) If whistles are fitted on a vessel at a distance apart of more than 100 metres, one whistle only shall be used for giving manoeuvring and warning signals.

Rule 36: Signals to attract attention

If necessary to attract the attention of another vessel any vessel may make light or sound signals that cannot be mistaken for any signal authorised elsewhere in these Rules, or may direct the beam of her searchlight in the direction of the danger, in such a way as not to embarrass any vessel. Any light to attract the attention of another vessel shall be such that it cannot be mistaken for any aid to navigation. For the purpose of this Rule the use of high intensity intermittent or revolving lights, such as strobe lights, shall be avoided.

Rule 37: Distress signals

When a vessel is in distress and requires assistance she shall use or exhibit the signals described in Annex IV to these Regulations.

9: The Small Print

Exemptions, specifications and technical details

Most of the small print is concerned with technical details that are mainly of interest to those concerned with designing a new ship or boat, or refitting an existing one.

The exception is Annex IV on page 70, which lists fifteen international distress signals – including the infamous "burning tar barrel" – and makes it illegal to misuse them.

PART E - EXEMPTIONS

Rule 38: Exemptions

Any vessel (or class of vessels) provided that she complies with the requirements of the International Regulations for Preventing Collisions at Sea, 1960 (a), the keel of which is laid or which is at a corresponding stage of construction before the entry into force of these Regulations may be exempted from compliance therewith as follows:

(a) The installation of lights with ranges prescribed in Rule 22, until 4 years after the date of entry into force of these Regulations.

(b) The installation of lights with colour specifications as prescribed in Section 7 of Annex I to these Regulations, until 4 years after the date of entry into force of these Regulations.

(c) The repositioning of lights as a result of conversion from Imperial to metric units and rounding off measurement figures, permanent exemption.

(d)

- (i) The repositioning of masthead lights on vessels of less than 150 metres in length, resulting from the prescriptions of Section 3(a) of Annex I to these Regulations, permanent exemption.
- (ii) The repositioning of masthead lights on vessels of 150 metres or more in length, resulting from the prescriptions of Section 3(a) of Annex I to these Regulations, until 9 years after the date of entry into force of these Regulations.

See Cmnd.2956 and Schedule 1 to the Collision Regulations (Ships and Seaplanes on the Water) and Signals of Distress (Ships) Order 1965 (S.I. 1965/1525)

(e) The repositioning of masthead lights resulting from the prescriptions of Section 2(b) of Annex I to these Regulations, until 9 years after the date of entry into force of these Regulations.

(f) The repositioning of sidelights resulting from the prescriptions of Sections 2(g) and 3(b) of Annex I to these Regulations, until 9 years after the date of entry into force of these Regulations.

(g) The requirements for sound signal appliances prescribed in Annex III to these Regulations, until 9 years after the date of entry into force of these Regulations.

(h) The repositioning of all-round lights resulting from the prescription of Section 9(b) of Annex I to these Regulations, permanent exemption.

ANNEX I : Positioning and technical details of lights and shapes

1. Definition

The term "height above the hull" means height above the uppermost continuous deck. This height shall be measured from the position vertically beneath the location of the light.

2. Vertical positioning and spacing of lights

(a) On a power-driven vessel of 20 metres or more in length the masthead lights shall be placed as follows:
   (i) the forward masthead light, or if only one masthead light is carried, then that light, at a height above the hull of not less than 6 metres, and, if the breadth of the vessel exceeds 6 metres, then at a height above the hull not less than such breadth, so however that the light need not be placed at a greater height above the hull than 12 metres;
   (ii) when two masthead lights are carried the after one shall be at least 4.5 metres vertically higher than the forward one.

(b) The vertical separation of masthead lights of power-driven vessels shall be such that in all normal conditions of trim the after light will be seen over and separate from the forward light at a distance of 1,000 metres from the stem when viewed from sea-level.

(c) The masthead light of a power-driven vessel of 12 metres but less than 20 metres in length shall be placed at a height above the gunwale of not less than 2.5 metres.

(d) A power-driven vessel of less than 12 metres in length may carry the uppermost light at a height of less than 2.5 metres above the gunwale. When however a masthead light is carried in addition to sidelights and a sternlight or the all-round light prescribed in Rule 23(c)(i) is carried in addition to sidelights, then such masthead light or all-round light shall be carried at least 1 metre higher than the sidelights.

(e) One of the two or three masthead lights prescribed for a power-driven vessel when engaged in towing or pushing another vessel shall be placed in the same position as either the forward masthead light or the after masthead light; provided that, if carried on the aftermast, the lowest after masthead light shall be at least 4.5 metres vertically higher than the forward masthead light.

(f) (i) The masthead light or lights prescribed in Rule 23(a) shall be so placed as to be above and clear of all other lights and obstructions except as described in sub-paragraph (ii).
   (ii) When it is impracticable to carry the all-round lights prescribed by Rule 27(b)(i) or Rule 28 below the masthead lights, they may be carried above the after masthead light(s) or vertically in between the forward masthead light(s) and the after masthead light(s) provided that in the latter case the requirement of Section 3(c) of this Annex shall be complied with.

(g) The sidelights of a power-driven vessel shall be placed at a height above the hull not greater than three-quarters of that of the forward masthead light. They shall not be so low as to be interfered with by deck lights.

(h) The sidelights, if in a combined lantern and carried on a power-driven vessel of less than 20 metres in length, shall be placed not less than 1 metre below the masthead light.
   When the Rules prescribe two or three lights to be carried in a vertical line, they shall be spaced as follows:
   (i) on a vessel of 20 metres in length or more such lights shall be spaced not less than 2 metres apart, and the lowest of these lights shall, except where a towing light is required, be placed at a height of not less than 4 metres above the hull;
   (ii) on a vessel of less than 20 metres in length such lights shall be spaced not less than 1 metre apart and the lowest of these lights shall, except where a towing light is required, be placed at a height of not less than 2 metres above the gunwale;
   (iii) when three lights are carried they shall be equally spaced.

(j) The lower of the two all-round lights prescribed for a vessel when engaged in fishing shall be at a height above the sidelights not less than twice the distance between the two vertical lights.

(k) The forward anchor light prescribed in Rule 30(a)(i), when two are carried, shall not be less than 4.5 metres above the after one. On a vessel of 50 metres or more in length this forward anchor light shall be placed at a height of not less than 6 metres above the hull.

3. Horizontal positioning and spacing of lights

(a) When two masthead lights are prescribed for a power-driven vessel, the horizontal distance between them shall not be less than one-half of the length of the vessel but need not be more than 100 metres. The forward light shall be placed not more than one-quarter of the length of the vessel from the stem.

(b) On a power-driven vessel of 20 metres or more in length the sidelights shall not be placed in front of the forward masthead lights. They shall be placed at or near the side of the vessel.

(c) When the lights prescribed in Rule 27(b)(i) or Rule 28 are placed vertically between the forward masthead light(s) and the after masthead light(s) these all-round lights shall be placed at a horizontal distance of not less than 2 metres from the fore and aft centreline of the vessels in the athwartship direction.

(d) When only one masthead light is prescribed for a power-driven vessel, this light shall be exhibited forward of amidships; except that a vessel of less than 20 metres in length need not exhibit this light forward of amidships but shall exhibit it as far forward as is practicable.

4. Details of location of direction-indicating lights for fishing vessels, dredgers and vessels engaged in underwater operations

(a) The light indicating the direction of the outlying gear from a vessel engaged in fishing as prescribed in Rule 26(c)(ii) shall be placed at a horizontal distance of not less than 2 metres and not more than 6 metres away from the two all-round red and white lights. This light shall be placed not higher than the all-round white light prescribed in Rule 26(c)(i) and not lower than the sidelights.

(b) The lights and shapes on a vessel engaged in dredging or underwater operations to indicate the obstructed side and or the side on which it is safe to pass, as prescribed in Rule 27(d)(i) and (ii), shall be placed at the maximum practical horizontal distance, but in no case less than 2 metres, from the lights or shapes prescribed in Rule 27(b)(i) and (ii). In no case shall the upper of these lights or shapes be at a greater height than the lower of the three lights or shapes prescribed in Rule 27(b)(i) and (ii).

5. Screens for sidelights

The sidelights of vessels of 20 metres or more in length shall be fitted with inboard screens painted matt black, and meeting the requirements of Section 9 of this Annex. On vessels of less than 20 metres in length the sidelights, if necessary to meet the requirements of Section 9 of this Annex, shall be fitted with inboard matt black screens. With a combined lantern, using a single vertical filament and a very narrow division between the green and red sections, external screens need not be fitted.

6. Shapes

(a) Shapes shall be black and of the following sizes:
   (i) a ball shall have a diameter of not less than 0.6 metre;
   (ii) a cone shall have a base diameter of not less than 0.6 metre and a height equal to its diameter;
   (iii) a cylinder shall have a diameter of at least 0.6 metre and a height of twice its diameter;
   (iv) a diamond shape shall consist of two cones as defined in (ii) above having a common base.

(b) The vertical distance between shapes shall be at least 1.5 metres.

(c) In a vessel of less than 20 metres in length shapes of lesser dimensions but commensurate with the size of the vessel may be used and the distance apart may be correspondingly reduced.

7. Colour specification of lights

The chromaticity of all navigation lights shall conform to the following standards, which lie within the boundaries of the area of the diagram specified for each colour by the International Commission on Illumination (CIE).

The boundaries of the area for each colour are given by indicating the corner co-ordinates, which are as follows:

(i) White

x	0.525	0.525	0.452	0.310	0.310	0.443
y	0.382	0.440	0.440	0.348	0.283	0.382

(ii) Green

x	0.028	0.009	0.300	0.203
y	0.385	0.723	0.511	0.356

(iii) Red

x	0.680	0.660	0.735	0.721
y	0.320	0.320	0.265	0.259

(iv) Yellow

x	0.612	0.618	0.575	0.575
y	0.382	0.382	0.425	0.406

8. Intensity of lights

(a) The minimum luminous intensity of lights shall be calculated by using

$I = 3.43 \times 10^6 \times T \times D^2 \times K^{-D}$

where I is luminous intensity in candelas under service conditions,

T is threshold factor 2 x 10-7 lux,

D is range of visibility (luminous range) of the light in nautical miles,

K is atmospheric transmissivity.

For prescribed lights the value of K shall be 0.8, corresponding to a meteorological visibility of approximately 13 nautical miles.

(b) A selection of figures derived from the formula is given in the following table:

Range of visibility (luminous range) of light in nautical miles D	Luminous intensity of light in candelas for K=0.8 I
1	0.9
2	4.3
3	12
4	27
5	52
6	94

Note: The maximum luminous intensity of navigation lights should be limited to avoid undue glare. This shall not be achieved by a variable control of the luminous intensity.

9. Horizontal sectors

(a)

(i) In the forward direction, sidelights as fitted on the vessel shall show the minimum required intensities. The intensities shall decrease to reach practical cut-off between 1 degree and 3 degrees outside the prescribed sectors.

(ii) For sternlights and masthead lights at 22.5 degrees abaft the beam for sidelights, the minimum required intensities shall be maintained over the arc of the horizon up to 5 degrees within the limits of the sectors prescribed in Rule 21. From 5 degrees within the prescribed sectors the intensity may decrease by 50 per cent up to the prescribed limits: it shall decrease steadily to reach practical cut-off at not more than 5 degrees outside the prescribed sectors.

(b)

(i) All-round lights shall be so located as not to be obscured by masts, topmasts or structures within angular sectors of more than 6 degrees, except anchor lights prescribed in Rule 30, which need not be placed at an impracticable height above the hull.

(ii) If it is impracticable to comply with paragraph (b) (i) of this section by exhibiting only one all-round light, two all-round lights shall be used suitably positioned or screened so that they appear, as far as practicable, as one light at a distance of one mile.

10. Vertical sectors

(a) The vertical sectors of electric lights as fitted, with the exception of lights on sailing vessels underway shall ensure that:

(i) at least the required minimum intensity is maintained at all angles from 5 degrees above to 5 degrees below the horizontal;

(ii) at least 60 per cent of the required minimum intensity is maintained from 7.5 degrees above to 7.5 degrees below the horizontal.

(b) In the case of sailing vessels underway the vertical sectors of electric lights as fitted shall ensure that:

(i) at least the required minimum intensity is maintained at all angles from 5 degrees above to 5 degrees below the horizontal;

(ii) at least 50 per cent of the required minimum intensity is maintained from 25 degrees above to 25 degrees below the horizontal.

(c) In the case of lights other than electric these specifications shall be met as closely as possible.

11. Intensity of non-electric lights

Non-electric lights shall so far as practicable comply with the minimum intensities, as specified in the table given in Section 8 of this Annex.

12. Manoeuvring light

Notwithstanding the provisions of paragraph 2(f) of this Annex the manoeuvring light described in Rule 34(b) shall be placed in the same fore and aft vertical plane as the masthead light or lights and, where practicable, at a minimum height of 2 metres vertically above the forward masthead light, provided that it shall be carried not less than 2 metres vertically above or below the after masthead light. On a vessel where only one masthead light is carried the manoeuvring light, if fitted, shall be carried where it can best be seen, not less than 2 metres vertically apart from the masthead light.

13. High Speed Craft*

(a) The masthead light of high-speed craft may be placed at a height related to the breadth of the lower than that prescribed in paragraph 2(a)(i) of this Annex, provided that the base angle of the isosceles triangles formed by the sidelights and masthead light, when seen in end elevation, is not less than 27°.

(b) On high-speed craft of 50 metres or more in length, the vertical separation between foremast and mainmast light of 4.5 metres required by paragraph 2(a)(ii) of this Annex may be modified provided that such distance shall not be less than the value determined by the following formula:

$$Y = \frac{(A + 17\psi)}{1000} C + 2$$

Where: Y is the height of the mainmast light above the foremast light in metres;
A is the height of the foremast light above the water surface in service condition in metres;
ψ is the trim in service condition in degrees;
C is the horizontal separation of masthead lights in metres.

*Refer to the International Code of Safety for High-Speed Craft, 1994 and the International Code of Safety for High-Speed Craft, 2000.

14. Approval

The construction of lights and shapes and the installation of lights on board the vessel shall be to the satisfaction of the appropriate authority of the State whose flag the vessel is entitled to fly.

ANNEX II: Additional signals for fishing vessels fishing in close proximity

1. General

The lights mentioned herein shall, if exhibited in pursuance of Rule 26(d), be placed where they can best be seen. They shall be at least 0.9 metre apart but at a lower level than lights prescribed in Rule 26(b)(i) and (c)(i). The lights shall be visible all round the horizon at a distance of at least 1 mile but at a lesser distance than the lights prescribed by these Rules for fishing vessels.

2. Signals for trawlers

(a) Vessels of 20 metres or more in length when engaged in trawling, whether using demersal or pelagic gear, shall exhibit:
   (i) when shooting their nets, two white lights in a vertical line;
   (ii) when hauling their nets, one white light over one red light in a vertical line;
   (iii) when the net has come fast upon an obstruction, two red lights in a vertical line.

(b) Each vessel of 20 metres or more in length engaged in pair trawling shall exhibit:
   (i) by night, a searchlight directed forward and in the direction of the other vessel of the pair;
   (ii) when shooting or hauling their nets or when the nets have come fast upon an obstruction, the lights prescribed in 2(a) above.

(c) A vessel of less than 20 metres in length engaged in trawling, whether using demersal or pelagic gear or engaged in pair trawling, may exhibit the lights prescribed in paragraphs (a) or (b) of this Section, as appropriate.

3. Signals for purse seiners

Vessels engaged in fishing with purse seine gear may exhibit two yellow lights in a vertical line. These lights shall flash alternately every second and with equal light and occultation duration. These lights may be exhibited only when the vessel is hampered by its fishing gear.

ANNEX III: Technical details of sound signal appliances

1. Whistles

(a) Frequencies and range of audibility

The fundamental frequency of the signal shall lie within the range 70 - 700 Hz. The range of audibility of the signal from a whistle shall be determined by those frequencies, which may include the fundamental and/or one or more higher frequencies, which lie within the range 180 - 700 Hz (+/-1%) for a vessel of 20 metres or more in length, or 180 - 2100 Hz (+/-1%) for a vessel of less than 20 metres in length and which provide the sound pressure levels specified in paragraph I(c) below.

(b) Limits of fundamental frequencies

To ensure a wide variety of whistle characteristics, the fundamental frequency of a whistle shall be between the following limits:

(i) 70 - 200 Hz, for a vessel 200 metres or more in length;
(ii) 130 - 350 Hz, for a vessel 75 metres but less than 200 metres in length;
(iii) 250 - 700 Hz, for a vessel less than 75 metres in length.

(c) Sound signal intensity and range of audibility

A whistle fitted in a vessel shall provide, in the direction of maximum intensity of the whistle and at a distance of 1 metre from it, a sound pressure level in at least one 1/3rd-octave band within the range of frequencies 180 - 700 Hz (+/-1%) for a vessel of 20 metres or more in length, or 180 - 2100 Hz (+/-1%) for a vessel of less than 20 metres in length, of not less than the appropriate figure given in the table below.

Length of vessel in metres	1/3rd-octave band level at 1 metre in dB referred to 2x10-5N/m^2	Audibility range in nautical miles
200 or more	143	2
75 but less than 200	138	1.5
20 but less than 75	130	1
	120 *	
Less than 20	115 †	0.5
	111 ‡	

* When the measured frequencies lie within the range 180 - 450 Hz
† When the measured frequencies lie within the range 450 - 800 Hz
‡ When the measured frequencies lie within the range 800 - 2100 Hz

The range of audibility in the table above is for information and is approximately the range at which a whistle may be heard on its forward axis with 90 per cent probability in conditions of still air on board a vessel having average background noise level at the listening posts (taken to be 68 dB in the octave band centred on 250 Hz and 63 dB in the octave band centred on 500 Hz). In practice the range at which a whistle may be heard is extremely variable and depends critically on weather conditions; the values given can be regarded as typical but under conditions of strong wind or high ambient noise level at the listening post the range may be much reduced.

(d) Directional Properties

The sound pressure level of a directional whistle shall be not more than 4 dB below the prescribed sound pressure level on the axis at any direction in the horizontal plane within ±45 degrees of the axis. The sound pressure level at any other direction in the horizontal plane shall be not more than 10 dB below the prescribed sound pressure level on the axis, so that the range in any direction will be at least half the range on the forward axis. The sound pressure level shall be measured in that 1/3rd-octave band which determines the audibility range.

(e) Positioning of whistles

When a directional whistle is to be used as the only whistle on a vessel, it shall be installed with its maximum intensity directed straight ahead. A whistle shall be placed as high as practicable on a vessel, in order to reduce interception of the emitted sound by obstructions and also to minimize hearing damage risk to personnel. The sound pressure level of the vessel's own signal at listening posts shall not exceed 110 dB (A) and so far as practicable should not exceed 100 dB (A).

(f) Fitting of more than one whistle

If whistles are fitted at a distance apart of more than 100 metres, it shall be so arranged that they are not sounded simultaneously.

(g) Combined whistle systems

If due to the presence of obstructions the sound field of a single whistle or one of the whistles referred to in paragraph (f) above is likely to have a zone of greatly reduced signal level, it is recommended that a combined whistle system be fitted so as to overcome this reduction. For the purposes of the Rules a combined whistle system is to be regarded as a single whistle. The whistles of a combined system shall be located at a distance apart of not more than 100 metres and arranged to be sounded simultaneously. The frequency of any one whistle shall differ from those of the others by at least 10 Hz.

2. Bell or gong

(a) Intensity of signal

A bell or gong, or other device having similar sound characteristics shall produce a sound pressure level of not less than 110 dB at a distance of 1 metre from it.

(b) Construction

Bells and gongs shall be made of corrosion-resistant material and designed to give a clear tone. The diameter of the mouth of the bell shall be not less than 300mm for vessels of 20 metres or more in length. Where practicable, a power-driven bell striker is recommended to ensure constant force but manual operation shall be possible. The mass of the striker shall be not less than 3 per cent of the mass of the bell.

3. Approval

The construction of sound signal appliances, their performance and their installation on board the vessel shall be to the satisfaction of the appropriate authority of the State whose flag the vessel is entitled to fly.

ANNEX IV: Distress signals

1. The following signals, used or exhibited either together or separately, indicate distress and need of assistance:

(a) a gun or other explosive signal fired at intervals of about a minute;
(b) a continuous sounding with any fog-signalling apparatus;
(c) rockets or shells, throwing red stars fired one at a time at short intervals;
(d) a signal made by radiotelegraphy or by any other signalling method consisting of the group • • • — — — • • • (SOS) in the Morse code;
(e) a signal sent by radiotelephony consisting of the spoken word "Mayday";
(f) the International Code Signal of distress indicated by N.C.;
(g) a signal consisting of a square flag having above or below it a ball or anything resembling a ball;
(h) flames on the vessel (as from a burning tar barrel, oil barrel, etc.);
(i) a rocket parachute flare or a hand flare showing a red light;
(j) a smoke signal giving off orange-coloured smoke;
(k) slowly and repeatedly raising and lowering arms outstretched to each side;
(l) the radiotelegraph alarm signal;
(m) the radiotelephone alarm signal;
(n) signals transmitted by emergency position-indicating radio beacons;
(o) approved signals transmitted by radiocommunication systems, including survival craft radar transponders.

2. The use or exhibition of any of the foregoing signals except for the purpose of indicating distress and need of assistance and the use of other signals which may be confused with any of the above signals is prohibited.

3. Attention is drawn to the relevant sections of the International Code of Signals, the Merchant Ship Search and Rescue Manual and the following signals:

(a) a piece of orange-coloured canvas with either a black square and circle or other appropriate symbol (for identification from the air);
(b) a dye marker.

10: Key Points

On one hand, simple paraphrases of the rules can be dangerously misleading. On the other, the full text of the rules is long and complicated. So here is a brief summary of the key points.

1. Keep a proper look-out
2. Maintain a safe speed
3. Assess the risk of any potential collision

- In open water, give way to anyone that is higher than you in the pecking order:
    - a vessel which you are overtaking
    - a vessel not under command
    - a vessel restricted in its ability to manoeuvre
    - a vessel constrained by its draught
    - a vessel engaged in fishing
    - a sailing vessel
    - a power-driven vessel
    - a seaplane or WIG craft (wing in ground-effect)
- When power-driven vessels meet:
    - in a head-on situation, both alter course to starboard
    - in a crossing situation, the one which sees the other on her starboard side must give way
- When sailing vessels meet
    - on opposite tacks, the one on port tack must give way
    - on the same tack, the windward one must give way
- In narrow channels, keep to starboard of the centre-line
- In separation schemes, follow the appropriate lane or cross at right angles
- Do not impede a vessel that is confined to a narrow channel or that is following a separation scheme
- In fog
    - sound the appropriate fog signal
        - 5 second blast every 2 minutes for vessels under power
        - Morse D every 2 minutes for vessels under sail
    - if you hear another vessel ahead, slow down or stop
    - if you detect a potential collision by radar, alter course to port if the other vessel is on your starboard quarter, otherwise alter course to starboard
- At night, display the correct lights:
    - sidelights and a sternlight for vessels under sail
        - do not confuse matters by adding extra lights
    - sidelights, a sternlight, and a masthead light for vessels under power (less than 50m in length)
        - sailing yachts under power should be particularly careful to ensure that the masthead tricolour is switched off when the masthead "steaming" light is switched on.
- When giving way:
    - Avoid crossing ahead of the other vessel
    - An alteration of course is generally more effective than a change of speed
    - Altering course to starboard is almost always better than altering course to port
    - Any change of course should be big enough to be obvious to the other vessel
- When standing on:
    - the rules say that a stand-on vessel *"**shall** keep her course and speed … until it becomes apparent to her that the vessel required to keep out of the way is not taking appropriate action"* : it is mandatory, not optional or advisory.

Index

Index

NOTES

Golden rule : Page 23.

Do not alter course to Port.

NOTES

Membership

Promoting and Protecting Boating

The RYA is the national organisation which represents the interests of everyone who goes boating for pleasure. The greater the membership, the louder our voice when it comes to protecting members' interests. Apply for membership today, and support the RYA, to help the RYA support you.

Benefits of Membership

- Special members' discounts on a range of products and services including boat insurance, books, charts, DVDs and class certificates
- Access to expert advice on all aspects of boating from legal wrangles to training matters
- Free issue of Certificate of Competence; increasingly asked for by overseas governments, holiday companies, insurance underwriters and boat hire companies
- Third Party insurance for windsurfing members
- Access to the wide range of RYA publications, including the RYA quarterly magazine
- E-newsletters, tailored to the type of boating you enjoy, to keep you up to date and give you the chance to join the debate on issues that affect you
- Regular offers in RYA Magazine
- ...and much more

Membership form opposite or join online at www.rya.org.uk

Visit our website for information, advice, members' services and web shop